Illustrator:
Howard Chaney

Editor:
Mary Kaye Taggart

Editorial Project Manager:
Karen J. Goldfluss, M.S. Ed.

Editor in Chief:
Sharon Coan, M.S. Ed.

Art Director:
Elayne Roberts

Associate Designer:
Denise Bauer

Cover Artist:
Larry Bauer

Product Manager:
Phil Garcia

Imaging:
David Bennett
Ralph Olmedo, Jr.

Cover Photos:
Images © 1995 PhotoDisc, Inc.

Publishers:
Rachelle Cracchiolo, M.S. Ed.
Mary Dupuy Smith, M.S. Ed.

W9-CZI-273

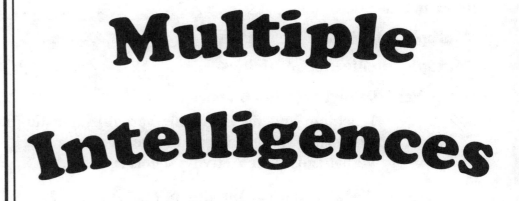

Multiple Intelligences Activities

(Grades K – 4)

Author:

Deirdré Korff Wilkens, M.A.

Teacher Created Materials, Inc.
P.O. Box 1040
Huntington Beach, CA   92647
ISBN-1-55734-398-5

©1996 Teacher Created Materials, Inc.

Made in U.S.A.

Table of Contents

Introduction

The education community has been clamoring for change for many years. Journal headlines suggest solutions. Politicians offer advice. Parents have their ideas of what should be done. There has been a growing trend in home schooling. Teachers are frustrated. Administration seems ineffective. All of this scurrying about has had dire effects on the very people we are trying to help—the students!

What is the solution? Many creative people have developed curricula, new approaches to learning, and new teaching techniques. Teachers often go to seminars heralding a "new, improved, and guaranteed successful" approach to classroom instruction. These presentations are often inspiring and full of great ideas. More often than not, teachers find themselves going back to their same classrooms, full of intent to implement these ideas, only to find the same textbooks, the same students, and the same old attitude about new ideas taking too much energy.

Teachers do not give up their quests for solutions, however. They keep searching, and once in awhile they find a theory, technique, or idea that really works for them, and they embrace it. Teachers adopted the theory of multiple intelligences because it did not require the discarding of previous ideas. Instead of starting over with some brand new plan, they could just supplement the good things they were already doing with ideas that would reach even more of their students.

The theory of multiple intelligences makes sense. It involves taking what teachers already do in the classroom and expanding that to enable them to be more successful with all of their students. We have all heard quotes about the fraction of our brains that we use. Studies have shown that only 10%–25% of the human brain is actually used. The theory of multiple intelligences ensures whole-brain learning. The use of different parts of the brain guarantees that teachers and students alike will use larger portions of their brains. The theory is encouraging and does not limit anyone to a preconceived notion of how smart they are. It stresses real-life learning, not the memorization of artificial, irrelevant snatches of information.

Celebrate learning with your students. Let them know that their potential is limitless. Help them to develop into successful, self-confident, well-rounded citizens by incorporating multiple intelligences into their lives. Putting this theory in practice has improved the personal and professional lives of teachers in amazing ways.

Theory of Multiple Intelligences

A Review

Traditionally, we have been led to believe that we are born with a certain potential for intelligence, and once we have gone through normal growth and education, we may reach and maintain that level of intelligence. This level can be determined by taking a pen-and-paper test using words, numbers, and maybe, a few pictures. This belief is not particularly encouraging.

In his book *Frames of Mind*: *The Theory of Multiple Intelligence* (Basic Books, 1983), Howard Gardner gives more hope with the theory of multiple intelligences. This theory proposes that people are not born with all of the intelligence they will ever have. Intelligence can be learned and improved upon throughout life. Everyone is intelligent in at least seven different ways and can develop each aspect of intelligence to an average level of competency (at the minimum). What an implication this theory has for students' success and self-esteem!

Intelligence, as defined by Gardner, is the ability to solve problems or fashion products that are valuable in one or more cultural settings. This allows for people in one culture to be just as intelligent as people in another. Problems or necessary products might vary from one culture to another. In a traditional Western culture it is understood that being able to use words and numbers is what makes a person smart. If students are not word or number smart, they, in effect, are not very intelligent by this measure. Gardner uses an example of people in the South Pacific. These people are considered smart if they are able to navigate by the stars. Numbers and words do not help them at all. Being space smart is more important to them.

Gardner has identified seven intelligences at this time, although he allows that there might be many more. Each of the defined intelligences has passed a test—eight criteria developed by Gardner and his associates. The criteria are summarized on the next page.

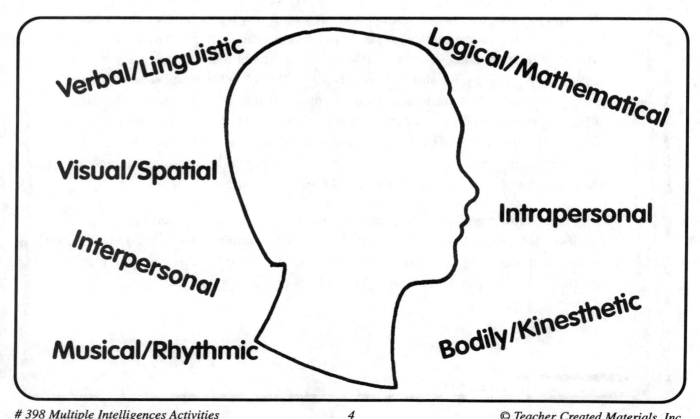

Theory of Multiple Intelligences *(cont.)*

Eight Criteria for Defining the Intelligences

- **Each of the intelligences can potentially be isolated by brain damage.** Gardner worked with people who had suffered brain damage, through accidents or illness, at the Boston Veterans Administration. He found that in some instances, brain damage could destroy a person's ability in one intelligence area and leave the other intelligences intact.

- **Each of the intelligences exists in exceptional people (savants or prodigies).** This means that there might be people who are exceptionally musically talented but who cannot get along well with others, have difficulty communicating, and have a hard time functioning in regular life experiences.

- **Each of the intelligences has a process of developing during normal child development and has a peak end-state performance.** For example, the verbal/linguistic intelligence presents itself in early childhood, while logical/mathematical intelligence peaks in adolescence and early adulthood.

- **Each of the intelligences is evidenced in species other than human beings.** We hear music and rhythm in bird songs. We find the visual/spatial intelligence in a bat's ability to navigate without eyesight.

- **Each of the intelligences has been tested using various measures not necessarily associated with intelligence.** For example, interpersonal and intrapersonal intelligences have been tested with the Coopersmith Self-Esteem Inventory. The Wechsler Intelligence Scale has been used to test logical/mathematical and linguistic/verbal abilities, as well as visual/spatial intelligence through picture arrangements in a subtest.

- **Each of the intelligences can work without the others being present.** For instance, a student who reads well, with good comprehension, might have trouble building a model using written directions because he/she cannot make a transfer between the two intelligences (verbal/linguistic and visual/spatial).

- **Each of the intelligences has a set of identifiable operations.** Gardner compares this to a computer needing a set of operations in order to function (like DOS). He suggests that each of the intelligences will one day be able to manifest itself in computer form because we can specify the steps necessary to do what each intelligence enables us to do.

- **Each of the intelligences can be symbolized or has its own unique symbol or set of symbols.** For example, bodily/kinesthetic intelligence uses sign language. Logical/mathematical intelligence uses computer languages. Interpersonal intelligence uses gestures and facial expressions.

Theory of Multiple Intelligences *(cont.)*

Identified Multiple Intelligences

The intelligences identified by Gardner all meet these eight criteria. He suggests that there might be others, and that is why his theory is called *multiple* intelligences and not *seven* intelligences. He has left room for more to be added.

The seven areas where intelligences have been identified are verbal/linguistic, logical/mathematical, visual/spatial, bodily/kinesthetic, musical/rhythmic, interpersonal, and intrapersonal.

The following is a brief description of each of the seven defined multiple intelligences. These intelligences will be described more completely under the specific headings throughout this book.

Multiple Intelligence	Description	Learning Style
Verbal/ Linguistic	This intelligence involves the use of language and words, whether written or spoken.	This type of learner likes to play with words in reading, writing, and speaking.
Logical/ Mathematical	This intelligence uses numbers, sequencing, and patterns to solve problems.	This type of learner likes to experiment with and explore numbers and patterns.
Visual/Spatial	This intelligence pertains to the use of shape, color, and form and the relationships among objects.	This type of learner likes to put his or her visualizations into drawing, building, designing, and creating.
Bodily/ Kinesthetic	This intelligence uses the body for self-expression. Coordination, dexterity, flexibility, and strength are all important in this intelligence.	This type of learner likes to move, touch, dance, play sports, do crafts, and learn through movement and touch.
Musical/ Rhythmic	This intelligence deals with pitch, tone, and rhythm.	This type of learner likes to sing, hum, play instruments, and generally respond to music.
Interpersonal	This intelligence is the ability to deal with other people. It involves one's ability to perceive what another person is thinking and feeling through body language and gestures.	This type of learner shares, compares, cooperates, has lots of friends, and learns with and from others.
Intrapersonal	This intelligence involves a self-knowledge, being able to identify one's own feelings and moods. Self-esteem and self-discipline are both particular to the intrapersonal intelligence.	This type of learner works alone at his or her own pace, producing original, unique work.

Identified Multiple Intelligences *(cont.)*

Everything we do falls under the intelligences listed on the previous page. It is very rare for one intelligence to work by itself. All of our activities involve a combination of intelligences. When a person runs, for example, he or she is using his or her bodily/kinesthetic and visual/spatial intelligences. It is very difficult to find an activity that purely uses only one intelligence.

As humans, we are like jigsaw puzzles. We have strengths and weaknesses in the intelligence areas. A person might be strong in two or more intelligence areas and still be able to develop the other areas to a high level.

Results of an intelligence test for the multiple intelligences could change from week to week, depending on the activities a person is involved with. During tax season, a person might score higher on the logical/mathematical intelligence area than at Christmas time. During the holiday season, a person could possibly score higher on the interpersonal intelligence because of the level of interaction with other people.

We constantly change. Gardner talks about proclivities or the potential to develop to a great degree in one of the intelligences. A person may or may not be an expert in an intelligence area where he/she has a proclivity, depending on whether he/she had the environmental stimulation necessary to develop in that area.

It is helpful to identify intelligences within ourselves and to understand how these intelligences are manifested in order to fully recognize them in our students. Understanding our own intelligences also helps us to concentrate on areas that might be low for us but are necessary for some of our students. To this end, a multiple intelligences inventory has been provided on the next page. The chart on page 10 summarizes the effect of each learning style on teaching.

After completing the inventory compare your inventory responses to the teaching styles chart to determine your learning style and its effect on your teaching.

MI Inventory for the Teacher

Check the statements below that apply to you in each intelligence area. If there are activities or preferences that are not referred to in the inventory, make a note of them under the appropriate heading.

Verbal/Linguistic

- ✓ I love to read books.
- ___ Words and languages fascinate me.
- ___ Spelling comes easily to me.
- ✓ I lose track of time when I am in a library or bookstore.
- ✓ I enjoy playing word games and puzzles.
- ✓ People enjoy listening to me tell stories.
- ___ I write about things I read and experience.
- ___ I can decipher and decode words I have never seen before.

Logical/Mathematical

- ___ Solving number probl_____ _ me.
- ___ M___ulating nu___

Musical/Rhythmic

- ✓ I sing along with the radio.
- ___ I am a member of a choir.
- ✓ I can play one or more musical instruments.
- ___ I work more effectively to background music.
- ___ It irritates me when someone sings off key.
- ___ My life would be dull without music.
- ✓ I have a good sense of rhythm.
- ✓ I often remember advertisement jingles.

Interpersonal

- ___ Spending time with friends helps me to unwind.
- I would _____ _er learn new _teria_ _th a

Theory of Multiple Intelligences *(cont.)*

MI Inventory for the Teacher

Check the statements below that apply to you in each intelligence area. If there are activities or preferences that are not referred to in the inventory, make a note of them under the appropriate heading.

Verbal/Linguistic

_____ I love to read books.
_____ Words and languages fascinate me.
_____ Spelling comes easily to me.
_____ I lose track of time when I am in a library or bookstore.
_____ I enjoy playing word games and puzzles.
_____ People enjoy listening to me tell stories.
_____ I write about things I read and experience.
_____ I can decipher and decode words I have never seen before.

Logical/Mathematical

_____ Solving number problems is easy for me.
_____ Manipulating numbers fascinates me.
_____ I can understand and interpret graphs easily.
_____ I often see patterns and sequences in things.
_____ I am good at explaining how to solve problems.
_____ Computers fascinate me.
_____ I expect everything to have a rational answer.

Visual/Spatial

_____ I often draw or doodle during staff meetings.
_____ I can express my mood effectively with color.
_____ I enjoy building things with blocks or other objects.
_____ A blank page and markers do not intimidate me.
_____ I enjoy watching television.
_____ I can draw pretty well.
_____ Spending time at an art museum relaxes me.

Bodily/Kinesthetic

_____ I am involved in a regular exercise program.
_____ I enjoy spending time in a park doing a physical activity.
_____ I willingly take an active part in school sports day.
_____ I cannot sit still for very long.
_____ I learn better when I am able to touch what I am learning about.
_____ I love spending time outdoors.
_____ I enjoy dancing.

Musical/Rhythmic

_____ I sing along with the radio.
_____ I am a member of a choir.
_____ I can play one or more musical instruments.
_____ I work more effectively to background music.
_____ It irritates me when someone sings off key.
_____ My life would be dull without music.
_____ I have a good sense of rhythm.
_____ I often remember advertisement jingles.

Interpersonal

_____ Spending time with friends helps me to unwind.
_____ I would much rather learn new material with a group of people.
_____ I often spend time chatting with friends.
_____ I am more productive when I work with a team.
_____ I very rarely do extracurricular activities alone.
_____ I often find myself in a group without consciously initiating the process.
_____ I am good at persuading people to do things my way.
_____ People come to me for comfort and/or moral support.

Intrapersonal

_____ Processing my thoughts alone is very important to me.
_____ I regularly think about my day and reflect on what I have accomplished.
_____ I can identify the things I am good at.
_____ I think that I am strong willed.
_____ I enjoy spending time by myself.
_____ Spending time with lots of people makes me nervous and agitated.
_____ I read or attend seminars for self-improvement.
_____ I have specific and realistic goals that I am working toward.

Theory of Multiple Intelligences *(cont.)*

This inventory is by no means an accurate picture of your intelligence profile. It does, however, give you an idea of where your personal interests lie. You probably found that you could mark several activities under each of the intelligences. Students possess each of the intelligences also. Just as you probably checked more under one heading than others, students will have some stronger areas than others. It is important that you work in each of the intelligence areas in your classroom, or have some help from parents or other teachers in areas where you do not feel as strong, so that you can reach and develop all the intelligences in all of your students.

Keep in mind that just because you did not check several options under a specific intelligence area does not mean that this is a weak area for you. Intelligences need to be fed through biological factors, as well as through environmental stimulation. You might have the biological heredity necessary to be strong in a specific intelligence area but might not have had the environmental stimulation. For example, perhaps you are very musically inclined but have not had access to a music instructor, and so this intelligence has not been given the opportunity to develop. You might even feel very uncomfortable using music in the classroom.

There are many ways the intelligences can be used or taught in the classroom. You can teach the intelligences as subjects. Traditional curriculum does this to an extent. For the verbal/linguistic intelligence, you teach language arts. For the logical/mathematical intelligence, you teach math, and so on. Visual/spatial, interpersonal, and intrapersonal intelligences may be addressed in even more limited terms, depending on your teaching style. These are not taught specifically. They generally fall under the hidden curriculum category.

Another way to use the intelligences in your classroom would be to create centers that cater to each of them. For the verbal/linguistic intelligence, you could have a writing and listening center with story starters and writing tools. A logical/mathematical intelligence center might include puzzles, sequencing activities, and problem-solving games. For the visual/spatial intelligence center, an art corner in which various art mediums are available works well. The musical/rhythmic intelligence center might include a music listening center and tools for creating music or lyrics. The bodily/kinesthetic intelligence center can be where you put your hands-on manipulatives. The interpersonal intelligence center can be a games area or any activity that involves cooperation between two or more students. The intrapersonal intelligence center could be as simple as a quiet corner where students can work in solitude.

A third way to use the multiple intelligences in the classroom is what this book will cover more comprehensively. This method is called teaching with the multiple intelligences.

Theory of Multiple Intelligences *(cont.)*

The Effects of Teachers' Learning Styles on Teaching

Learning Style	Effect on Teaching
The Verbal/Linguistic Learner	The teacher who is a linguistic learner stresses a curriculum based on language—reading, writing, and speaking. The whole-language approach is a natural one for this teacher. Students with more concrete learning styles may have a difficult time in this atmosphere unless the teacher stays alert to their needs.
The Logical/Mathematical Learner	The teacher who is a logical/mathematical learner tends to concentrate on concepts that are both logical and abstract. This teacher will need to make a deliberate effort to focus on the fact that it is appropriate for students to be artistic and to think in intuitive leaps.
The Visual/Spatial Learner	The teacher who is a spatial learner will provide a great learning environment for those who have traditionally been called visual learners. The artistic students will do well in this classroom. This teacher will need to build in adequate opportunities for students who are linguistic learners and for those who feel artistically inhibited.
The Bodily/Kinesthetic Learner	The teacher who is a kinesthetic learner will have a classroom full of things to manipulate and will probably encourage experiential learning. The classroom will be full of movement, and it may be a challenge to both the logical learner and the intrapersonal learner.
The Musical/Rhythmic Learner	The musical/rhythmic learner has been recognized as a separate type only recently. The teacher who is a musical learner will tend to have a relaxed classroom but may find it harder to relate to those students who are not "in tune with" music.
The Interpersonal Learner	The teacher who is an interpersonal learner generally uses cooperative learning in the classroom. Students in this teacher's classroom will not only feel free to interact but will also be expected to. This is the perfect classroom for the extrovert. This kind of teacher should try to cultivate respect and tolerance for the students who really need to be alone in order to create, to learn, or just to be.
The Intrapersonal Learner	There are probably not many teachers who are true intrapersonal learners. Those who are will have probably learned to use other styles in public and save this style for personal, creative times. A teacher who understands this style will be a great support for the student who has trouble functioning in groups.

Teaching with the Multiple Intelligences

You are already teaching with the multiple intelligences. The purpose of this section is to enable you to take a look at the students in your classroom in a new light. Are you reaching all of your students all of the time? How about some of your students all of the time? Would you like to reach all of your students most of the time?

Consider Your Teaching and Learning Styles

Now that you know what the multiple intelligences are, take a survey of your teaching style. Refer to the chart on page 10 for information on the effects a teacher's learning style may have on his or her teaching. Every time you do an activity, analyze it for which intelligences it targets. Think about the past week and do a mental checklist of all of the intelligences you have used. Chances are you will have used each of them to a degree, but, depending on your grade level, 75% or more of your activities will be verbal/linguistic, logical/mathematical, and, maybe, some interpersonal. (Lower grade teachers do use more of the intelligences due to the nature of your curriculum.) Your goal should be to use the intelligences equally, or as close to equally as you can comfortably get. Use the multiple intelligences (MI) calendar (page 13) to keep a realistic record of your activities.

Using the range of intelligences will also help you to find out what intelligence strengths your students have. Watch how their eyes shine when you hit their strong intelligences! Make a note of their strengths so you can target their weaknesses through their strong intelligences.

MI Weekly Calendar

Use this calendar to keep track of the teaching strategies you use in your weekly classroom planning.

Monday	Tuesday	Wednesday	Thursday	Friday	MI
					Verbal/Linguistic
					Logical/Mathematical
					Visual/Spatial
					Bodily/Kinesthetic
					Musical/Rhythmic
					Interpersonal
					Intrapersonal

Include the Multiple Intelligences in Your Lessons

The remaining sections of this book provide lesson plan ideas that will help you to have a wide range of activities in each of the intelligences. They are by no means the only activities to be used. It is hoped that these activities will get your creativity flowing and that you will come up with many more ideas on your own.

Teaching students about their intelligence strengths helps them to be self-advocates in their learning. They can internalize how they learn, which will help them cope with the teaching styles of teachers who might not be aware of the multiple intelligences. However, teaching students about the intelligences might not be viable, depending on the specific group you are dealing with, their age, or the point at which you are during the school year.

You already teach with the intelligences. These activities can help to broaden your teaching strategies palette and help you to reach all of your students more of the time. In each category you will find activities to help develop the students' weak intelligences through the use of their strong intelligences.

How to Use This Book

Under each of the multiple intelligence (MI) headings you will find a definition and description of the specific intelligence. Also included are activities that help you to teach with the intelligences, as well as about the intelligences. There will be lesson planning ideas which will help you to create your own lessons under each intelligence. For the students in your room who might have a weakness in the specific intelligence areas, and for the enrichment of others, you will find ways to access each of the intelligences through other intelligences. These strategies will be in the forms of career lists, field trips, biographies, displays and bulletin boards, games, and literature through which students will be able to learn. We will be using strong intelligence areas to access the weaker areas. For example, if a student has a difficult time with mathematics but is a strong bodily/kinesthetic learner, activities are identified that will help the student learn to do math by using his or her body.

At the beginning of each intelligence section are parts of an instructional unit that will help you to teach your students about their multiple intelligences. This unit is in the form of a story for the students, a child-size definition, and activities that will teach them about the intelligence, using activities of that intelligence. There are also letters to parents that will help them understand the different ways their children are smart, and the letters include activities that they can do at home to encourage and facilitate the development of each of the intelligences. At the end of each section are ways by which knowledge can be assessed using the intelligence areas.

This is truly a resource book, one from which you can glean ideas. It is not intended to be taught from as a textbook. Find the activities and ideas that work for you. Once you become more aware of the intelligences and your use of them in the classroom, you will be able to develop your own lesson plans and have your own ideas about what activities fit into each category. Keep in mind that just because an activity is listed under one intelligence area does not mean it cannot be used in another. Pure-form intelligence activities are difficult to come by. Most of what we do fits into two or more intelligence areas. You might find similar activities listed under several intelligence areas.

Student Activity

At the beginning of each activity page is a symbol identifying the intelligence highlighted in the activity. The symbols are as follows:

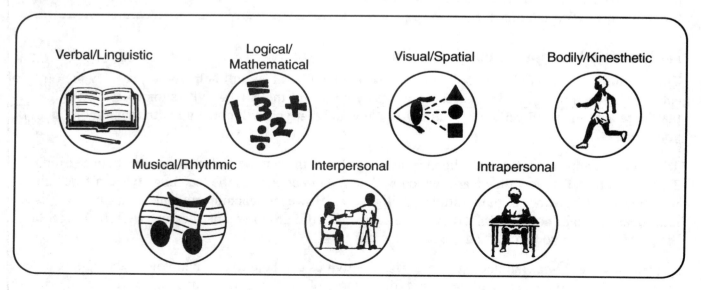

Each activity within a multiple intelligence section is written for a specific grade level. To determine the grade level of an activity, refer to the first page of each section.

MI Weekly Calendar

Use this calendar to keep track of the teaching strategies you use in your weekly classroom planning.

Monday	Tuesday	Wednesday	Thursday	Friday	MI
					Verbal/Linguistic
					Logical/Mathematical
					Visual/Spatial
					Bodily/Kinesthetic
					Musical/Rhythmic
					Interpersonal
					Intrapersonal

Letter to Parents

Dear Parents,

Among the many things we are learning and reinforcing in our classroom this year is the idea that we are intelligent. We will be exploring the many different ways in which we are smart, based on a theory by Howard Gardner.

In his theory of multiple intelligences, Gardner says that we are all smart in at least seven different ways. We are smart with words, numbers, pictures, music, our bodies, our friends, and with ourselves. We are all smart in all seven areas. Some of us might be more developed in some intelligence areas, and others will be more developed in other areas. The great news is that we can all cultivate all seven of our intelligences.

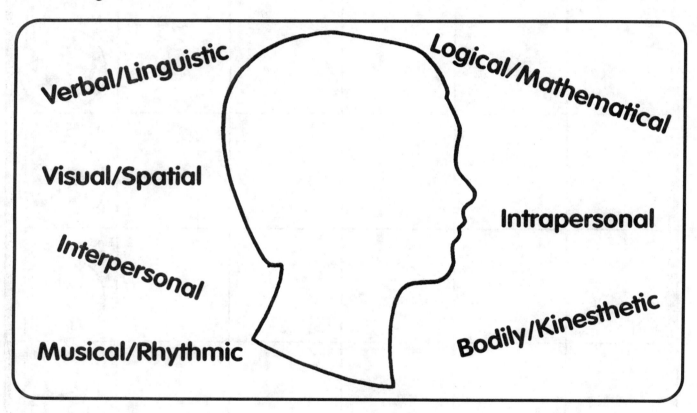

We will be doing many exciting things with these different ways of being smart. If you would like to find out more about this, please feel free to contact me or come by our classroom.

You will be receiving more letters about the different ways we are smart as the year progresses. In these letters you will find out what we are doing to develop all of our intelligences and also what activities you can do at home to help develop the intelligences.

We are enjoying the celebration of all of our intelligences.

Thank you for helping us!

Sincerely,

_____

(your child's teacher)

Multiple Intelligence Assessment

An Introduction

With a new way of teaching and learning should come a new way of assessing. We certainly would show ourselves in a poor light if we introduced our students to the wide variety of activities by which we can learn to solve problems and create products only to turn around and test this knowledge and skill with the same limiting, traditional method of assessment.

Fortunately for teachers of lower grades, this does not require a huge paradigm switch. We need to be aware, however, of the effects our assessment methods, have on our students. In the traditional curriculum and assessment methods students develop a level of paranoia towards assessment. This gives students an artificial learning environment where they learn to simply pass a test instead of developing themselves. Traditional assessment also limits teachers in what they do in the classroom. Many teachers, without consciously being aware of it, focus their teaching on a narrow area to ensure that the curriculum covers what will be tested.

There are many ways in which traditional assessment is limiting to students, where MI assessment (authentic assessment) can come to the rescue. Traditional assessment brings the multidimensional personalities and abilities of children to an inaccurate collection of grades. These grades cause incredible levels of stress on students, which affects them negatively. With grades come the norm or standard which unfairly forces the failure of a few students, concentrating on what the students did wrong as opposed to focusing on what positive abilities and skills they possess.

Traditional assessment also shows itself unauthentic in that it tests on a limited basis. Students are not able to bring prior knowledge and problem-solving skills to the assessment. They are not permitted to clarify their thoughts. They are forced to think artificially.

Virtually at no time are we tested or assessed in a real-life situation (such as on the job) where we are not allowed to bring prior experience and knowledge with us and discuss with our assessor our ideas and knowledge. With standardized tests, however, the test base covers a very limited area of knowledge, where students either know the material or they do not. This approach also forces a barrier between learning and assessment. Instead of using the results as a means by which to grow, they are the end of a set of instructions, and students have no recourse. Authentic assessment puts as much emphasis on the learning *process* as it does on the end result.

Multiple Intelligence Assessment *(cont.)*

The list of harmful effects from traditional assessment can go on, but that is not the purpose here. Authentic assessment allows students to celebrate what they know. It has a positive focus and encourages students to explain, justify, and use their minds to solve problems and create products. It lends itself to higher-level thinking, which is much more productive than the dead-end thinking that traditional assessment requires. MI assessment also encourages cooperative effort, rather than isolating students unnaturally to regurgitate information. Students are able to identify their own growth because authentic assessment allows them to see the progress they have made when compared to their earlier abilities, not compared to what other students are able to do. Each student is very different and should be allowed to solve problems and create products in his or her individual style.

What Is Authentic Assessment?

There are only two main areas of authentic assessment. These two components can be achieved through a variety of methods. The most essential ingredient in authentic assessment is *observation*. Watching the process by which students do various tasks and how they interact with classmates gives a much clearer picture of their skills and knowledge than could any traditional written assessment. The other ingredient, then, would be *recording* these observations, that is, documenting the students' progress and abilities. This documentation can take many forms. Teachers who are not familiar with the process might feel intimidated at first, but if you start the process in small, manageable steps, it will not seem as daunting. Pick the ideas and options that feel right for you and use these ideas as stepping stones to ideas of your own. Experiment until you find what suits you the best. This kind of assessment is part of the teaching/learning process, part of your everyday life. If you can incorporate this into your days now, report card week will not be nearly as stressful. Your work will be done. For some this process will not be new at all.

Observations Recording Options

This is just a sampling of the options available for documentation. Find the methods and materials that are most compatible with your style and personality.

Multiple Intelligence Assessment *(cont.)*

Descriptive Records

Keep a three-ring binder with a section for each of your students. Record events and progress as you observe them. This can include academic information, peer relations, use of materials, and other appropriate information for individual students. Students' behavior can be recorded on a log form (page 20).

Sample Files

This is a file that students can keep as easily as the teacher. (Give them part of the responsibility!) This file could include samples of work, or photocopies of work, done by individual students in math, language arts, art, etc. Photographs of large projects that cannot be placed in a file can accurately record your observations and could be included in the sample files for individual students.

Video and Audio Recordings

These can be used to record the process by which students do their work. They could include reading selections, oral presentations, peer relations, musical endeavors, etc.

Student Journals, Charts, and Calendars

Giving students the responsibility to record their own development could extend to journals and charts. Journals might include descriptions of what the students have done in the classroom and their feelings about their experiences. Diagrams, brainstorm lists, and spontaneous entries can be included along with required entries. Students can chart their progress on individual records. This could include mastery of various skills, books read, steps in a process, etc. Students can keep records of their activities in school on monthly calendars. The journals, charts, and calendars can be kept in a single folder for each student and collected at the end of a designated time period.

Checklists

With an established list of skill mastery requirements, a simple checklist can be kept to record which students have mastered which skills. This could also be done to check for steps in a learning process through which students must move. It will keep you in touch with what your students are doing and let you know who needs specific help and in which areas they need it.

Multiple Intelligence Assessment *(cont.)*

Tests and Standardized Tests

These can be used in informal settings to find out about an individual student's abilities in specific areas. Standardized test administration guidelines should be reviewed, however, to allow students to express why they chose various options and to give them an opportunity to dialogue about the process which they take to reach their conclusions.

Interviews

Talking with students about what they have experienced and learned in the classroom is an effective way to evaluate their understanding and knowledge of their learning environment. In these informal discussions the teacher can also establish what interests and abilities the students would like to explore beyond what they have already done. Anecdotal records of these interviews should be included in your notebook.

These observations can be accumulated in a student "processfolio" that will document a learning process for each student. Under each intelligence area throughout the book there are ideas for documenting specific intelligences, as well. This documentation can also be included in the processfolio.

All of these options are fine and good, but Americans (in general) often have a need for more concrete evidence of assessment. To accomplish this, or to make educators, parents, and administrators more comfortable with this new process, teachers might consider letting students choose the method by which they will be tested. For example, after working through a certain unit students might choose three (or another designated number) of the intelligence areas through which they will demonstrate an understanding of the concepts presented. The forms on pages 22 and 23 are examples by which students might indicate their preferences. This allows for authentic assessment to take place in a more controlled manner. These forms can be used as contracts of learning between the students and the teacher. Students will be able to use their strengths to solve problems or create products. (The form on page 22 is better for grades K–2 than the one on page 23.) Another option might be for the teacher to ask a specific question or pose a specific problem which students would need to solve, but they could choose the method by which to prove their skill or knowledge. These are all generic ideas through which assessment can take place.

As mentioned earlier, it is beneficial for the teacher to identify his or her students' strong intelligence areas. By doing this, the teacher can target weaker areas through students' strengths. The remaining sections of this book include ideas for accessing each intelligence through the other intelligence areas.

Multiple Intelligence Assessment *(cont.)*

In dealing with assessment, there are ways to use the formats we are familiar and comfortable with. Changing our focus and approach might help us to move from traditional assessment to authentic assessment. Evaluate your current methods and take the following into consideration when deciding on the assessment strategies you feel ready to implement. Internalizing a new definition of test might help you here.

A test or quiz structure should be considered when genuine and accurate assessment is your goal. This includes letting students know (in advance) what material they are expected to demonstrate their abilities in (to the extent of giving students a copy of the test at the beginning of the instruction period).

The testing environment should encourage the learning process instead of being the end result of learning. To do this, students should be able to explore various ways of producing the desired results. Their (test) efforts will be discussed and evaluated on an ongoing basis. They will have the opportunity to keep working on a project or list of criteria until the desired learning has taken place.

The design of the tests will demonstrate a focus on understanding, rather than mere parrot-like learning. To do this, real-life learning must take place, that is, learning beyond classroom work. There should be a connection between what is being learned in the classroom and what it is necessary to know in the real world. As such, tests can no longer be solely paper-and-pencil instruments. Students should, rather, have the opportunity to prove their knowledge and understanding through hands-on activities that demonstrate their skills. Students should have an understanding of how this learning relates to the world around them.

The evaluation of students' abilities demonstrated through their products should be in accordance with standards and goals set by the school. The evaluation of any project should be done in a way that does show priority for single intelligence areas. This might require the involvement of community members who have developed a high level of performance in the various intelligence areas. Core knowledge and understanding of the learning process, as well as the end result, should be the basis of the evaluation. Having students dialogue about their evaluations might bring clarification when necessary.

Behavior Observation Record

Student: _____ Grade: _____

Observation Period: _____

Plot the level of interest the student appears to have in each of the following categories, using a check mark or X. This observation does not need to take place at one sitting but should be a record of a specific time period (for example, a one-week period).

	Low Interest ↓	High Interest ↓

Verbal/Linguistic:

Enjoys presenting ideas by talking or writing | - |

Enjoys words by reading, writing, and/or talking | - |

Is not too shy to express self orally in public | - |

Uses words carefully in dealing with sensitive situations | - |

Effectively uses and understands age-appropriate humor | - |

Is a persuasive speaker | - |

Has a well-developed personal vocabulary | - |

Logical/Mathematical:

Able to see sequence and put random things in order | - |

Can recognize and understand patterns | - |

Is able to quantify objects easily | - |

Easily solves problems or puzzles | - |

Uses strategies and formulas to solve problems | - |

Is good at characterizing and classifying objects | - |

Is capable of higher-order thinking and reasoning | - |

Visual/Spatial:

Can reproduce objects with various media | - |

Spends large amounts of time drawing or doodling | - |

Learns easily when using visual aids | - |

Uses paints, clay, and other media for creative expression | - |

Can solve or use age-appropriate mazes and maps | - |

Has active imagination and enjoys pretending | - |

Can create objects by following directions | - |

Behavior Observation Record *(cont.)*

	Low Interest	High Interest

Bodily/Kinesthetic:

Enjoys moving around the classroom	I - - - - - - - - - - - - - - - - - - - I	
Expresses self with body movement/gestures	I - - - - - - - - - - - - - - - - - - - I	
Shows good coordination and skill in games	I - - - - - - - - - - - - - - - - - - - I	
Is good at using hands to create or fix things	I - - - - - - - - - - - - - - - - - - - I	
Chooses to play games like charades	I - - - - - - - - - - - - - - - - - - - I	
Enjoys showing people how to do things	I - - - - - - - - - - - - - - - - - - - I	
Happily takes part in exercise routines	I - - - - - - - - - - - - - - - - - - - I	

Musical/Rhythmic:

Works well when listening to music	I - - - - - - - - - - - - - - - - - - - I	
Sings or hums while playing and working	I - - - - - - - - - - - - - - - - - - - I	
Often taps pencil, ruler, feet, or fingers	I - - - - - - - - - - - - - - - - - - - I	
Easily remembers advertisement jingles and tunes	I - - - - - - - - - - - - - - - - - - - I	
Makes up nonsense tunes, songs, and rhymes	I - - - - - - - - - - - - - - - - - - - I	
Recognizes notes/tones in nonmusical situations	I - - - - - - - - - - - - - - - - - - - I	
Enjoys a variety of music	I - - - - - - - - - - - - - - - - - - - I	

Interpersonal:

Enjoys a meaningful family relationship	I - - - - - - - - - - - - - - - - - - - I	
Has friends outside of immediate family group	I - - - - - - - - - - - - - - - - - - - I	
Spends lots of class time discussing ideas with others	I - - - - - - - - - - - - - - - - - - - I	
Can involve others in a discussion	I - - - - - - - - - - - - - - - - - - - I	
Perceptive to feelings portrayed by body language	I - - - - - - - - - - - - - - - - - - - I	
Plays fairly and effectively in team situations	I - - - - - - - - - - - - - - - - - - - I	
Seems to be a leader in games and activities	I - - - - - - - - - - - - - - - - - - - I	

Intrapersonal:

Can identify causes of personal feelings and moods	I - - - - - - - - - - - - - - - - - - - I	
Asks many how and why questions	I - - - - - - - - - - - - - - - - - - - I	
Enjoys working alone in relative quiet	I - - - - - - - - - - - - - - - - - - - I	
Can express self in many different ways	I - - - - - - - - - - - - - - - - - - - I	
Does not worry about what others think	I - - - - - - - - - - - - - - - - - - - I	
Is perceptive and intuitive	I - - - - - - - - - - - - - - - - - - - I	
Is motivated and has good concentration skills	I - - - - - - - - - - - - - - - - - - - I	

To Show That I Know . . .

To show that I know _____

In some of the boxes below, describe how you will prove what you know.

I Will Use . . .

WORDS	NUMBERS	PICTURES
BODY	MUSIC	FRIENDS	SELF

Signed:

_____ (student)

_____ (teacher)

22

I Know My Stuff!

To show what I know,_____

_____ **I will . . .**

(Check one.)

_____ write a story, essay, or report.
_____ design a flyer, brochure, or advertisement.
_____ keep a journal, scrapbook, or diary.
_____ build a model or create an exhibit.
_____ give a speech, talk, or live presentation.
_____ teach it to another student.
_____ create drawings, sketches, or diagrams.
_____ create a chart, graph, or other analysis.
_____ create a rap or other song about the topic.
_____ produce a video or radio segment.
_____ design a mural, mobile, or 3-D illustration.
_____ participate in a group debate or discussion.
_____ collect music and songs about the topic.
_____ interview someone and record my findings.
_____ set up and perform an experiment.
_____ develop a group play or musical.
_____ create and complete a simulation.
_____ other (Check with your teacher.)

Here is a brief description of what I intend to do.

_____

_____

_____

_____

_____

Signed: _____ _____
(student) (teacher)

Verbal/Linguistic Intelligence

Table of Contents

Grade Level Suggestions for Activity Sheets

Activity Sheet Title	Page	Grade Level(s)
People and Words	43	K
At the Library	44	K
Word Search	45	1
About the Book	46	1
Using Your Word Intelligence	47	1
When I Use My Word Intelligence	48	2
At the Bookstore	49	2
Many Ways of Being Smart	50	2–3
Hidden Abilities	51	2–3–4
About the Topic	52	2–3
Taking Sides	53	3
The Note	54	3
Joking Around	55	3–4
Details, Details, Details	56	3–4
Book Report	57	3–4
Very Puzzling	58	3–4
Teaching an Alien	59	3–4
What's Important	60	3–4
Power Writing	61	3–4
Imagine . . .	62	4
Using Your Verbal/Linguistic Intelligence	63	4
What Happened Next?	64	4

Verbal/Linguistic Intelligence

Description

The verbal/linguistic intelligence is used in formal and informal speech and conversation. It is found anytime people put their thoughts on paper, whether in letters to friends or in creative writing. Storytelling and humor involving a play on words or twists of the language are also products of the verbal/linguistic intelligence. Understanding and using analogies, metaphors, similes, good grammar, and syntax are evidence of the verbal/linguistic intelligence in practice.

Students who are strong in the verbal/linguistic intelligence think in words and are good with language. They enjoy reading, writing, telling stories and jokes, and playing word games. They are effectively taught with books, tapes, writing stations, discussions, debates, and stories.

Development

The development of the verbal/linguistic intelligence begins in infancy when children babble. It grows into single word statements when children are around eighteen months old. By age two, many children are able to talk in simple sentences. Language continues to explode in early childhood. Four- and five-year olds are able to tell stories about life—real and imagined. Beyond this basic grasp of language skills, students have to specifically be taught the intricacies of their home language (depending on where they are being brought up). While almost everybody goes through similar developmental stages, some people take longer to master this intelligence than others. By the time students are through with the primary grades, however, they generally have a fairly equal ability in this intelligence area. The verbal/linguistic intelligence remains strong through adulthood and old age.

Parents' Letter

Dear Parents,

One of the many ways that we know we are smart is with the use of words. We are able to use words to express ourselves in speaking and in writing. We started developing this intelligence when we were just babies as we babbled and cooed. It continued to develop as we started using single words and then short sentences. This intelligence has continued to explode for us. We are very fascinated by words, and there are still so many to learn!

We are going to be spending some time finding out more about this intelligence, and we will work on strengthening it. We can strengthen and develop this intelligence by reading books and learning our vocabulary and spelling words. There are many other enjoyable things to do also:

- ◆ Games like *Spill and Spell* and *Scrabble Jr.* help us.
- ◆ Games like *Trivia* that require us to remember things are good.
- ◆ Word searches and crossword puzzles help us learn.
- ◆ Discussions at the table about different topics are beneficial.
- ◆ Learning a new word every week and trying to work it into conversation is a stimulating way for the family to learn together.
- ◆ Jokes and stories keep us in words (and stitches).
- ◆ Reading and understanding comic strips, jokes, and puns helps to develop our knowledge of words.

We hope you spend time developing this intelligence together as a family. Enjoy our rich language and one of our many ways of being smart. Until next time . . .

Sincerely,

_____

(your child's teacher)

Teaching Students About the Verbal/Linguistic Intelligence

Chapter One

Teacher Note: This is the first chapter of a seven-chapter story. There is a chapter at the beginning of each of the remaining sections in this book. These chapters are meant to be read aloud to students to introduce each of the intelligences. They are each followed by a children's definition of the intelligence and a suggested activity.

Melanie and Roger Burns lived in a place where it rained a lot. Many days they would sit inside and grumble because they did not have anything to do. Well, that was not really true. They had a lot of things to do, but you know how tired you get of reading your books and playing with your toys when all you really want to do is go outside and play, but you cannot because it is too wet.

On a particular day like this, they sat looking out of the window, trying to think of new things to do. They even asked their mother, Mrs. Burns, for suggestions.

Mrs. Burns said, "You should be able to think of something; you're smart kids."

But Melanie and Roger grumbled that their minds had turned to mud from all of the rain.

"That's not true!" said Mrs. Burns. "You are actually smart in at least *seven* ways!"

"What ways?" Melanie asked.

"Well, why don't you find out?" suggested Mrs. Burns.

So Melanie and Roger thought long and hard about how they could possibly be smart in *seven* ways, when they could not even think of *one* thing to do! While they were looking out the window, trying to think of how they were smart, Roger noticed several snails on the sidewalk.

"Hey!" he said. "Look at all of those snails! I wonder what they're doing out in the rain."

Roger and Melanie talked about it for awhile, and then Melanie decided she was going to write a story about the snails. Melanie was in third grade, so she could write pretty well. Roger was in first grade and could write some words, but writing was a little hard for him. However, they both sat down with some paper and pencils. Roger wrote what words he could, and Melanie helped him write some words that he could not. When Melanie was too busy writing her own story, Roger just drew little pictures to help him remember what words he meant to write. They had been writing for quite a while when Mrs. Burns came in to see what was keeping them so quiet after all of the grumbling she had been hearing. She got a big grin on her face when she saw them writing. She did not say anything but went into the kitchen to start preparing dinner. Melanie read her story to Roger. They laughed at it together. It was not a story that could really happen, but it was very cute. Then Roger read his story to Melanie. She thought his story was pretty good too. They decided to write a letter to their Grandma and send her the stories they had written.

Teaching Students About the Verbal/Linguistic Intelligence *(cont.)*

When they were finished with their letters, they went to ask Mrs. Burns for an envelope and a stamp.

"Well," said Mrs. Burns, "I see you found one of the ways in which you're smart!"

"No," said Melanie, "we got tired of thinking about that, so we decided to write stories instead."

"By doing that," said Mrs. Burns, "you can see that you are smart with words!"

Melanie and Roger never imagined they were smart with words.

"But anyone can tell a story," said Roger.

"That's right," said Mrs. Burns, "everyone can be word smart!"

They helped Mrs. Burns set the table for dinner, and they left feeling pretty good about themselves.

Without even being told how to do it, they had found out that they were word smart. When Mr. Burns came home for dinner, they heard their mom say, "Melanie and Roger discovered their verbal/linguistic intelligence today."

Dad seemed really impressed. They did not know what that meant. They felt good enough about just being word smart.

Children's Definition:

> Being *word smart* means that you can talk, write, and listen to words. Anytime you tell stories, write letters, tell or laugh at jokes, read books, or use language in any way, you are using your *word skills*. Everyone is word smart!

Activity:

Write or tell a story, real or imagined, about a time you went on a treasure hunt and had to follow word puzzles or riddles to find the treasure.

Other activities can be found under "Lesson Planning Activities" on page 29, and "Activities Across the Grade Levels" starting on page 30.

Lesson Planning Activities

The following is a list of activities that you can use when creating a verbal/linguistic lesson or when you are planning to strengthen this intelligence. Use these activities in combination with those listed under other intelligences to develop a well-rounded curriculum.

- Biographies
- Book Reporting
- Brainstorming
- Cartoons
- Creative Writing
- Debates
- Diaries
- Discussions
- Essays
- Explanations
- Feelings
- Formal Speaking
- Humor
- Impromptu Speaking
- Journal Writing
- Letter Writing

- Library Research
- Lists
- Persuasion
- Poetry
- Publishing
- Reading
- Recall of Verbal Information
- Reports
- Speaking
- Surveys
- Storytelling/Creation
- Tape Recording
- Telling Jokes
- Vocabulary
- Writing Words

Verbal/Linguistic Activities Across the Grade Levels

Predictions:

After reading a book or part of a book, have the students predict what might happen next.

Students in kindergarten and the first grade can do this by sharing their predictions with the class.

Students in the second, third, and fourth grades might share their predictions with friends.

Students in the third and fourth grades can write their predictions down and then share them with friends or in groups.

Word Games and Puzzles:

In kindergarten and the first grade, students enjoy playing word guessing games. The teacher can give clues to a certain word that might be part of the current curriculum. For instance, if the class is studying about families, the teacher might say,

> "I'm thinking of a word that tells about an important person who works hard to support, or help support, the family. This person will often work away from the home to earn money. He and Mom have to make many important decisions about what is good for the family. Who is he?"

> (Dad)

Older students will enjoy the same game if the clues are more difficult.

Children also enjoy word puzzles. Students may complete or create word puzzles using their vocabulary or spelling words. These puzzles might range from scrambled word puzzles or word searches for younger students to crossword puzzles for advanced students. Have the students solve puzzles created by classmates.

I jyonede sthi meag

mimseylne!

(I enjoyed this game immensely!)

Daily New Word:

Teach your students a new vocabulary word each day.

Kindergartners and first graders can learn the word and its meaning verbally. Let them practice saying the word and give them plenty of examples of sentences in which the word is used. Then work the word into your instruction during the day. When the students hear the word, have them raise their hands. When you acknowledge their correct identification of the word, have them repeat it to you in a sentence (either the one you used or one they create that shows understanding). Reward them when they correctly identify and use the new word.

Second through fourth graders can use the same activity as above, as well as work the word into their own conversations. Write the word on the board and have students write it and its definition into student dictionary notebooks/journals. Reward their use of the current word, as well as previous words, in their daily writing and conversations.

Same Sound Tongue Twisters:

Create a brainstorm list of words with your students. All the words on one list should begin with the same sound. For example, your beginning sound might be PL. After you have a list of words, use them to make a tongue twister. "Please place the plate on the platter while you play with the plunger on the playground." This can be used with writing skills, reading, handwriting practice, phonics, etc.

Literature:

All books with text fit into the verbal/linguistic intelligence area because they deal with the use of language. The following list is a limited selection dealing with play on words, special descriptive language, humor, and other classroom favorites. Books are an effective way to access other intelligences when students are strong in the verbal/linguistic intelligence.

- *Alexander and the Terrible, Horrible, No Good, Very Bad Day,* by Judith Viorst: Aladdin, 1987
- *Bennett Cerf's Book of Riddles,* by Bennett Cerf: Beginner, 1967
- *Caddie Woodlawn,* by Carol Ryrie Brink: Aladdin, 1990
- *Caps for Sale,* by Esphyr Slobodkina: Scholastic, 1989
- *Cloudy with a Chance of Meatballs,* by Judith Barrett: Aladdin, 1982
- *Crow Boy,* by Taro Tashima: Puffin, 1976
- *Eight Ate: A Feast of Homonym Riddles,* by Marvin Terban: Clarion, 1982
- *Freckle Juice,* by Judy Blume: Four Winds Press, 1984
- *Harriet the Spy,* by Louise Fitzhugh: Trophy, 1990
- *Haunted House Jokes,* by Louis Phillips: Puffin, 1988
- *The House at Pooh Corner,* by A. A. Milne: Puffin, 1992
- *Jokes for Children by Children,* by Marguerite Kohl and Fredrica Young: FS & G, 1983
- *Just So Stories,* by Rudyard Kipling: Viking, 1993
- *Millions of Cats,* by Wanda Gag: Sandcastle, 1977
- *Miss Nelson Is Missing,* by Harry Allard: Houghton Mifflin, 1993
- *The Phantom Tollbooth,* by Norton Juster: Knopf, 1993
- *Rabbit Hill,* by Robert Lawson: Puffin, 1977
- *Sarah, Plain and Tall,* by Patricia MacLachlan: Cornerstone Books, 1988
- *Windsongs and Rainbows,* by Burton Albert: Simon & Schuster, 1993
- *What Do You Say, Dear?* by Sesyle Joslin: HarpC Child Books, 1986
- *Where Does the Trail Lead?* by Burton Albert: Simon & Schuster, 1993
- *Words with Wrinkled Knees,* by Barbara Juster Esbensen: Crowell Jr., 1987
- Various books by Bill Peet

Accessing Verbal/Linguistic Intelligence Through Logical/Mathematical Intelligence

Outline:

Grades 3–4: Create an outline of a topic of your choice (review of a book, favorite hobby, field trip experience, etc). This might be done as a class activity to begin with so that students can get a feel for how to outline. Start by listing three subtopics. Each subtopic should then have three details to support it.

Code Language:

Grades K–2: Have the class create a code by which they can tell a story they have recently read. The code could be as simple as Indian-style pictographs. Review the story by deciphering the coded version.

Grades 3–4: Students might work in pairs or groups to create a code by which to retell a story. Be sure that they write keys for their codes so that classmates can decipher the codes.

Differences/Similarities:

Use butcher paper or flip charts on which your class can create charts. Have students note the similarities and differences between two characters in a book, or between two books, or between two students in the class. Venn diagrams work well for making comparisons.

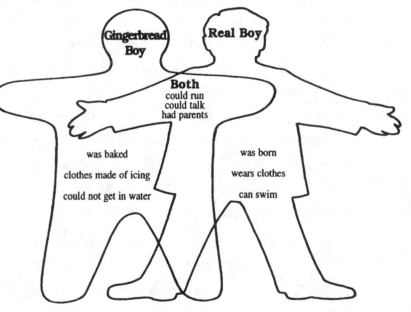

Pattern Recognition:

Many books have patterns with repetitive language. Read part of a repetitive book to the students. Ask the students to identify the pattern and predict what might come next.

There are many early childhood picture books that can be used in even the upper grades when dealing with word study and prediction. A good example of a repetitive book is *Over in the Meadow* (Illustrated by Ezra Jack Keats. Scholastic, Inc., 1971—original version by Olive A. Wadsworth).

Another example of patterns in literature can be found in rhyming books. Bill Peet uses a lot of rhyme in his writing, which appeals to students of all ages.

There are many patterns within language. These patterns can be seen and heard. Have the students identify patterns in words and sounds. Help them to recognize that certain letter patterns produce certain sounds. This activity will help students with decoding words in reading.

Accessing Verbal/Linguistic Intelligence Through Visual/Spatial Intelligence

Story Illustrations:

While a story is being read, or after it is read, have students draw a picture to illustrate a character, plot, or event in the story. Older students might create a storyboard to show a sequence of events in their drawings.

If you are reading a longer book to your students, they might create a picture book about it. When your book is finished they will have a pictorial account of what the book is about.

Pictionary:

Visual/spatial learners will enjoy learning their vocabulary by playing a version of the classic game *Pictionary.* One student will draw pictures to get teammates or classmates to guess a vocabulary word. The student who correctly identifies the vocabulary word is the next one to have a turn at drawing.

Displays:

Visual/spatial students like to see finished products. Create classroom displays that show items created with words. These displays might include published stories that the students have written or classroom books. Visual/spatial students might be responsible for creating classroom bulletin boards.

See the bulletin board idea below and the one on the following page for other verbal/linguistic displays.

Accessing Verbal/Linguistic Intelligence Through Visual/Spatial Intelligence *(cont.)*

After reading a familiar story, ask the students to illustrate their favorite parts or assign each student a part. They should label their illustrations to explain what part of the story they are illustrating. With the help of the class, put the illustrations in chronological order. Display them on the bulletin board.

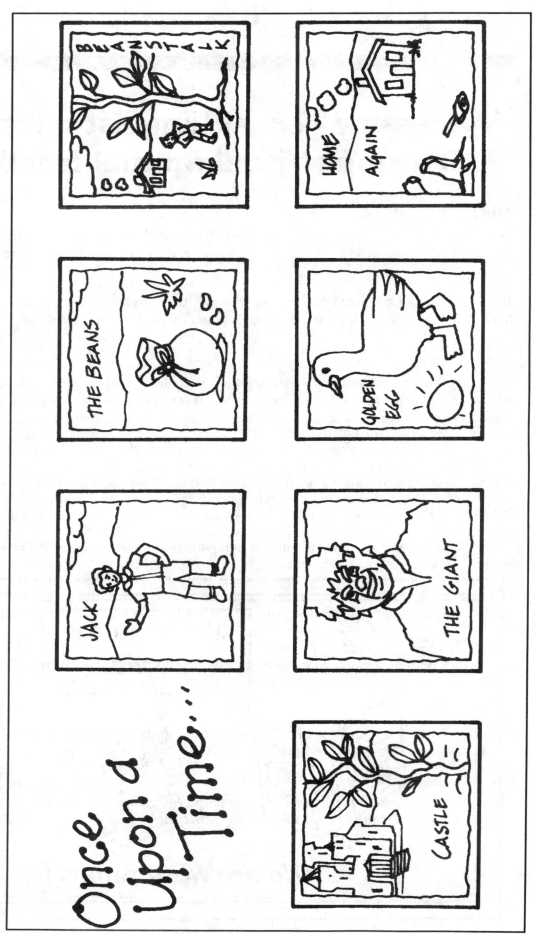

34

Accessing Verbal/Linguistic Intelligence Through Bodily/Kinesthetic Intelligence

Field Trips:

Bodily/kinesthetic students learn through moving and touching. Use the list of verbal/linguistic oriented careers (page 41) to find places in your community where your students could experience hands-on learning. Some examples might be a trip to a publisher, newspaper office, or radio station (where they do news reports, etc.).

Body Language:

Help students to see that they can express themselves through nonverbal body language. Exercises to practice this might be done by asking students to show, without sound, how a bored person might look. How would a happy person look? How would an excited person look? How would an important person look?

Sign Language:

Many teachers have already incorporated sign language into their language programs. This is an excellent tool for teaching bodily/kinesthetic language. Many classroom management tasks can be accomplished with signs. Students might invent their own signs for going to the bathroom, for showing they are finished with their assignments, or for asking to sharpen their pencils.

Body Vocabulary:

For those students who wiggle through lessons and have difficulty remembering content words, assigning actions to the words might help them remember them more effectively. For example, if the word is "rain," students might make themselves into raindrops so that they will remember the word. Be sure the students *see* the word written down and *hear* the word spoken along with the action of *doing* the word. They will associate the words with the actions and be more successful at remembering them. Let the students come up with their own actions for their words to allow for internalized learning.

Pasta Words:

Let students do their writing with dry pasta letters. This works especially well with spelling words. Let them keep a permanent record of their weekly list by gluing the letters onto graph paper.

Story Acts:

Students could act out a story while it is being read. Assign various characters to different students. This works especially well if the students are already familiar with the story and its characters.

Body Alphabet:

Master the alphabet by assigning a body movement or gesture to each letter. Practice using the alphabet by having students spell their names with their bodies.

Charades:

One at a time, let students play the parts of characters in a book you are reading. Let the class guess which characters they are pretending to be. Play charades across the curriculum by having students pretend to be vocabulary words, spelling words, animals, parts of a flower, punctuation marks, a person in history, or various professional people.

Accessing Verbal/Linguistic Intelligence Through Musical/Rhythmic Intelligence

Poetry:

Musical/rhythmic students learn by sound and rhythm. Using different intonations and inflections in your teaching voice will help to access these students. These students will respond positively to poetry. Rhyming words are particularly interesting. Have the musical/rhythmic students write their spelling words into a poem or ask them to find words that rhyme with their spelling/vocabulary words.

Choral Reading:

Reading might be difficult for musical/rhythmic students until they are able to sing their stories. Assign different parts to different groupings of students, give them time to rehearse, and then watch them perform their lessons.

Morse Code:

Learn Morse Code with your students and have them transmit sentences, using their vocabulary words. To transmit, they may tap out the code on their desks or make up oral versions. Have classmates receive and interpret the messages and check with the transmitter for accuracy.

A	• –	O	– – –	3	• • • – –
B	– • • •	P	• – – •	4	• • • • –
C	– • – •	Q	– – • –	5	• • • • •
D	– • •	R	• – •	6	– • • • •
E	•	S	• • •	7	– – • • •
F	• • – •	T	–	8	– – – • •
G	– – •	U	• • –	9	– – – – •
H	• • • •	V	• • • –	10	– – – – –
I	• •	W	• – –	, (comma)	– – • • – –
J	• – – –	X	– • • –	. (period)	• – • – • –
K	– • –	Y	– • – –	– (hyphen)	– • • • • –
L	• – • •	Z	– – • •	(parenthesis)	– • – – • –
M	– –	1	• – – – –	' (apostrophe)	• – – – – •
N	– •	2	• • – – –	underline	• • – – • –

Accessing Verbal/Linguistic Intelligence Through Musical/Rhythmic Intelligence *(cont.)*

Repetitive Action Stories:

Find read-aloud books with actions that repeat. Assign a certain rhythmic hand clap or percussion sound to each action.

When you read each action, have the students perform their assigned sound. They will be forced to listen to the language in order to play their instruments!

Chants:

There are many recordings of multiplication chants and raps. Many parts of the curriculum can be learned this way. Classroom and safety rules can be committed to memory with chants. Advertising is successful many times due to the chants or jingles associated with various products. Older students can create their own raps or chants. Younger students will follow your lead with fingerplays and nursery rhymes.

As a class, students might write a jingle or chant to advertise a special book after it is read a few times. Ask your students to write and perform these jingles for other classes to encourage them to read the book, as well.

Sound Effects:

Let students choose a story to perform. They will be responsible for any sound effects the story might need to make it come alive. Have them perform their stories for their classmates or for other classes. Younger students might collaborate with the teacher to create one sound-effect story together.

Sound Punctuation:

Assign each punctuation mark a sound, for instance, a squeak for each comma and a grunt for each period. Have students read a paragraph or story by reading the words and sounding each punctuation mark they come across (similar to Victor Borge's famous comedy routine).

Accessing Verbal/Linguistic Intelligence Through Interpersonal Intelligence

Sharing:

Grades K–2: After you have read a story to the class, have the students pair up and retell the story to their partners. Provide your students with a story starter and then ask them to finish the story for their teammates. Trade off so that everyone has an opportunity to tell a story.

Grades 3–4: When students write creative stories or poems, have them share these with their peers. Peer evaluation in the editing process will also encourage these social students to improve their verbal/linguistic skills. Having students read to each other encourages them to use their linguistic intelligence in a less threatening environment.

Grades K–4: Have students read aloud to each other in cross-age pairs. This gives them a greater opportunity to have oral reading practice and allows them to share their love of reading with partners. Arrange with teachers of other grade levels to spend a few periods a week with cross-age buddies.

Joint Story Creation:

Grades K–4: Provide students with a story starter. Let the plot thicken in your introduction. Turn the story over to pairs or groups of students. Have the students take turns developing and solving the story. Use a timer and have the partner tell his or her story until the timer rings. The next student then may take a turn at advancing the story. Use shorter time periods for younger students.

"Emotional" Reading:

Grades K–2: Have students repeat a given phrase with different tones of voice. Instruct them to let their voices show pride, annoyance, excitement, jealousy, happiness, fear, curiosity, or worry.

Give them an example by repeating the following phrases, showing some of the above emotions:

> "My little sister is making a lot of new friends."

> "My mother is starting her new job today."

> "My grandma gave this to me for my birthday."

Grades 3–4: Let the students read short poems, expressing various emotions by their intonations and expression. Model this by using the above phrases.

Rain
The rain is raining all around,
It falls on field and tree,
It rains on the umbrellas here,
And on the ships at sea.

by Robert Louis Stevenson

Accessing Verbal/Linguistic Intelligence Through Interpersonal Intelligence *(cont.)*

Games:

Games can provide learning in social settings. The following lists are examples of games that will help in the development of the verbal/linguistic intelligence.

- spelling games, such as crossword puzzles, word jumbles, *Junior Scrabble,* and *Spill* and *Spell*
- word guessing and vocabulary games, such as hangman and *Balderdash*
- impromptu speaking games, such as speaking about a random item found in the classroom
- linguistic twist games, such as riddles, pun wars, or "Can you top this?" joke telling

Group Projects:

For older students, projects can be divided into parts, and each part can be assigned to a different student. When the students are finished with their parts, these parts together will make a whole.

For younger students, round-robin story telling is a good group project. It might even be the retelling of a classroom story. Have one student tell a part of the story and then call on a classmate to continue for awhile, and then that student calls on another classmate, and so on.

Cooperative Groups:

In his book *Seven Pathways of Learning**, David Lazear outlines jobs that members of a verbal/linguistic cooperative group might have.

Reader is responsible for reading the written material that is necessary to complete a lesson the group is working on.

Secretary takes notes on the group's work and does any writing the lesson requires.

Speller checks all of the group's products for correct spelling.

Reporter communicates the results of the group's work to the rest of the class.

Historian keeps a record of key events that occur while the group is working.

Poet writes poems or limericks about the group and the work it has done in a lesson.

Comedian entertains the group with jokes, puns, and humorous comments about the lesson.

Memory jogger helps the group create gimmicks for remembering a lesson.

Debater takes an opposing position in a discussion to promote thinking and discussion.

Storyteller tells others stories about the high and low points that occurred as the group worked on a task.

*From *Seven Pathways of Learning,* David Lazear. Tucson, Arizona: Zephyr Press, 1994.

Accessing Verbal/Linguistic Intelligence Through Intrapersonal Intelligence

Autobiographical Stories:

Grades K–2: Ask your students to tell an autobiographical story called "My Life…This Week." Have them continue with a sequel called "My Life in the Next Five Years."

Grades 3–4: Have your students write or tell an autobiographical story called "My Life…So Far." Ask them to continue with a sequel called "My Life in the Next Five Years."

Character Identification:

After reading a book, encourage your students to identify with the characters. Ask students questions such as these:

- If you could be any one of the characters, which one would you choose? Why?
- Which character would be your best friend? Why?
- Which character do you dislike? Why?

Opposite Arguments:

Ask each student to select an opinion he/she has (the best school lunch, the best book, etc.) and ask him/her to pretend to actually think the opposite of that opinion. Have your students argue for the opposite position.

Extend this activity by having other students play the devil's advocates and forcing the arguing student to defend the opposite opinion.

Biographies:

There are many people who use their verbal/linguistic intelligence to do great things. Listed below are some well-known experts in their fields. Have the students read these biographies or those of other similar historical figures.

- Agatha Christie
- Edgar Allan Poe
- Rudyard Kipling
- William Shakespeare
- T.S. Eliot

For younger students, however, it might be more meaningful to see and meet someone who uses the verbal/linguistic intelligence. Invite someone from your community who uses this intelligence in his/her workplace to come and speak with your class. It is suggested that you use the list of careers on the next page and the phone book to help find an individual.

Accessing Verbal/Linguistic Intelligence Through Intrapersonal Intelligence *(cont.)*

Software:

Students who have strong intrapersonal intelligence do well when they are left to do work at their own pace. Working on a computer enables them to do self-paced work and have the help they might need without having to interact with other influences.

- Word processing programs, such as *Word Perfect* or *Microsoft Word*
- Typing tutors, such as *Mavis Beacon Teaches Typing*
- Desktop publishing, such as *Publish It!*
- Electronic libraries, such as *World Library*
- Interactive storybooks, such as *Storyweaver* and *Just Grandma and Me*
- Word games, such as *Missing Links*
- IBM EduQuest's *Writing to Read*
- Wings for Learning/Sunburst's *Muppet State*
- National Geographic's *Kids Network*
- Apple's *HyperCard*
- IBM's *LinkWay*

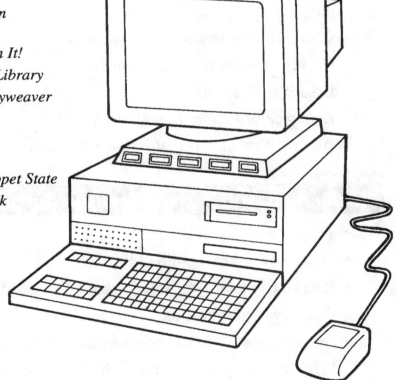

Careers:

- Archivist
- Author
- Comedian
- Curator
- Journalist
- Language Teacher
- Librarian
- Newscaster
- Novelist
- Playwright
- Poet
- Proofreader
- Public Speaker
- Radio Announcer
- Secretary
- Speech Pathologist
- Storyteller
- Typist
- Writer

Verbal/Linguistic Assessment

Verbal/Linguistic Processfolio Inclusions:

- Invented writing (for younger grades)
- Word/sentence writing
- Evidence of learned spelling and vocabulary words
- Student-created poetry
- Writing process notes—prewriting, editing, rough draft, final product
- Best writing (can be replaced with new writing as time goes by)
- Descriptions and reports of investigations and discoveries
- Audio/video tapes of verbal activities (storytelling, debates, discussions, reading, etc.)
- Checklists for reading skill mastery
- Copies of journal or diary entries
- Essays and reports
- Evidence of memory recall activities
- Any product of a verbal/linguistic lesson

Evaluation with Verbal/Linguistic Intelligence:

- Tell a story to explain . . . .
- Write how you would feel if . . . .
- Record (on a tape recorder) what you thought of . . . .
- Give a verbal report on . . . .
- Create a poem, riddle, or joke that shows you understand . . . .
- Write a word problem in which you demonstrate (math skill) . . . .
- Write a newspaper article about the time when (history/social studies) . . . .
- Participate in a debate or discussion about the issue . . . .
- Retell the story we read.
- Explain how you would . . . .
- Write an imaginary interview between . . . .
- Use your spelling/vocabulary words to create a limerick, poem, or riddle.
- Use any activity that requires the use of language as a response or product.

People and Words

Circle the pictures of people using words.

At the Library

Look at the picture below. Think of words to describe what is happening in the
picture. Write the words on the lines below.

_____

_____

_____

_____

_____

_____

 **Name**

Word Search

You are smart in many ways. Look for words about the different ways you are smart in the word search below. Find the words from the word bank. The words can be found across (↔) or down (↓).

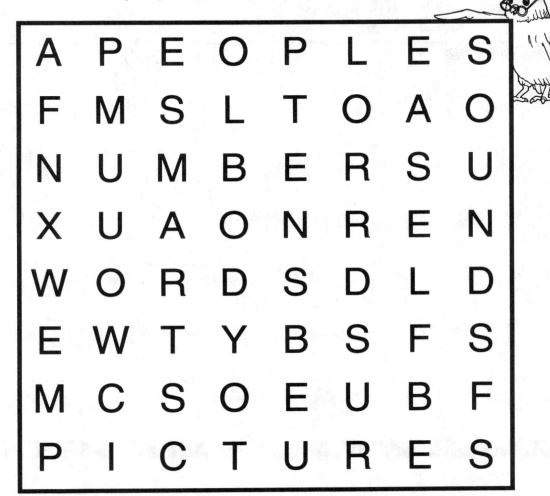

A	P	E	O	P	L	E	S
F	M	S	L	T	O	A	O
N	U	M	B	E	R	S	U
X	U	A	O	N	R	E	N
W	O	R	D	S	D	L	D
E	W	T	Y	B	S	F	S
M	C	S	O	E	U	B	F
P	I	C	T	U	R	E	S

WORD BANK

| WORDS | BODY | NUMBERS | SELF |
| PICTURES | PEOPLE | SOUNDS | SMART |

About the Book

Think of a book you have read or one that someone has read to you. Draw a picture about the book and then write some words to tell about the book.

Words about the book:_____

_____

_____

_____

_____

 **Name**

Using Your Word Intelligence

Think about different things you do that use your word talents. Write words which tell when you use this word intelligence.

 **Name**

When I Use My Word Intelligence

Using the word ideas in the list, write sentences about when you use
your word intelligence on the lines below.

> **Word Ideas**
>
> | reading | writing | books |
> | jokes | poems | stories |
> | telling | listening | spelling |

_____

_____

_____

_____

_____

_____

_____

_____

_____

 **Name**

At the Bookstore

Look at the picture below. What is happening? Write sentences on the lines below to describe the picture.

_____

_____

_____

_____

_____

_____

Many Ways of Being Smart

Look at the two big words below. These words mean "many ways of being smart." Use the letters in these words to make as many other words as you can. Try to make your words at least three letters long.

MULTIPLE INTELLIGENCES

Name

Hidden Abilities

The words below are all about the different ways that you are smart. Find the words from the word bank in the word search. The words can be found going up (↑), down (↓), across (↔), and diagonally (↘).

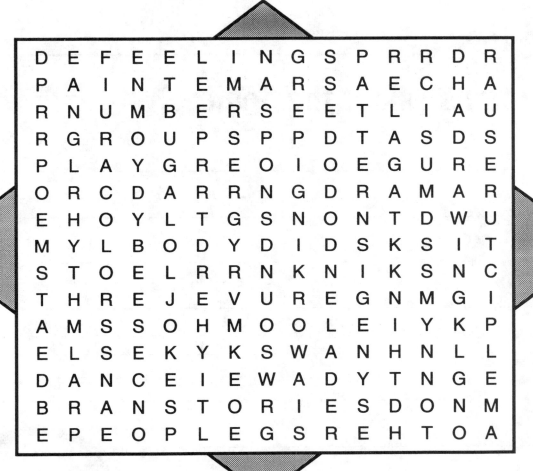

```
D  E  F  E  E  L  I  N  G  S  P  R  R  D  R
P  A  I  N  T  E  M  A  R  S  A  E  C  H  A
R  N  U  M  B  E  R  S  E  E  T  L  I  A  U
R  G  R  O  U  P  S  P  P  D  T  A  S  D  S
P  L  A  Y  G  R  E  O  I  O  E  G  U  R  E
O  R  C  D  A  R  R  N  G  D  R  A  M  A  R
E  H  O  Y  L  T  G  S  N  O  N  T  D  W  U
M  Y  L  B  O  D  Y  D  I  D  S  K  S  I  T
S  T  O  E  L  R  R  N  K  N  I  K  S  N  C
T  H  R  E  J  E  V  U  R  E  G  N  M  G  I
A  M  S  S  O  H  M  O  O  L  E  I  Y  K  P
E  L  S  E  K  Y  K  S  W  A  N  H  N  L  L
D  A  N  C  E  I  E  W  A  D  Y  T  N  G  E
B  R  A  N  S  T  O  R  I  E  S  D  O  N  M
E  P  E  O  P  L  E  G  S  R  E  H  T  O  A
```

Word Bank

Numbers	Paint	Jokes	Music
Dance	Working	Colors	Stories
Body	Patterns	Groups	Drawing
Sounds	Play	Others	People
Feelings	Sports	Problems	Think
Poems	Singing	Drama	
Pictures	Mind	Rhythm	

 **Name**

About the Topic

Think about something you recently heard or learned about. Now think about questions you have about that topic. Write the questions on the lines below.

Topic: _____

Questions About the Topic:

_____

_____

_____

_____

_____

_____

_____

_____

_____

_____

 **Name**

Taking Sides

Think about a discussion or argument you recently had with someone. Write the topic of your discussion on the first line. Think of facts for your side of the discussion. Write them on one side. Then think of facts for the other side of the discussion. Write them on the other side. Which side has the most facts?

The discussion was about . . . _____

_____

_____

My Facts:	Other Facts:
_____	_____
_____	_____
_____	_____
_____	_____
_____	_____
_____	_____
_____	_____
_____	_____
_____	_____
_____	_____
_____	_____
_____	_____

The Note

Rochelle found an old bottle at the beach. There was a cork in it. When Rochelle pulled the cork out, she found a note written by someone far away.

Write who the note was from and about the journey of the bottle.

Joking Around

Think of some jokes you have heard about animals. Write those jokes on this page.

_____

_____

_____

_____

_____

_____

_____

_____

_____

_____

_____

_____

_____

_____

_____

Details, Details, Details

Think of a story you recently heard or read and really enjoyed. How well do you remember the details of the story? Without looking at the story, rewrite it here. Include as many details as you can.

Title: _____

_____

_____

_____

_____

_____

_____

_____

_____

_____

_____

_____

_____

_____

_____

_____

_____

_____

_____

_____

 **Name**

Book Report

Title: _____

Author: _____

Illustrator: _____

Number of Pages: _____

Favorite Characters: _____

_____

_____

_____

Favorite Event: _____

_____

_____

_____

Tell something you would have done differently from the way a character did it.

_____

_____

_____

_____

_____

Write a short advertisement of the book for your classmates.

_____

_____

_____

_____

_____

Very Puzzling

Use the word bank to complete the sentences. Then use the clues to fill in the crossword puzzle.

Word Bank:

word
problems
number
sing
self
groups
picture
people
body
intelligence

Across

1 The use of color is part of your _____ intelligence.
3 People who use their _____ intelligence a lot like to work by themselves.
4 People who like to _____ use their music intelligence.
6 You use your number intelligence when you solve _____ .
9 Catching a ball, running, and jumping rope all use your _____ intelligence.

Down

2 _____ is another word for your abilities.
5 When you play in _____ you use your people intelligence.
7 Recognizing patterns uses your _____ intelligence.
8 When you tell a story, you are using your _____ intelligence.
10 When you recognize what others are feeling, you are using your _____ intelligence.

 **Name**

Teaching an Alien

Think of an everyday thing you do, like washing dishes, brushing your teeth, making a sandwich, etc. Explain how to do this regular and ordinary thing to an alien who might never have even heard about the process. Be as complete and specific as you can.

This is an explanation of . . .

_____

_____

_____

_____

_____

_____

_____

_____

_____

_____

_____

_____

_____

_____

_____

_____

_____

_____

_____

 **Name**

What's Important

Think about something that is really important to you. It might not be important to many other people, but it is to you. Write about this important thing. What makes it important? Is it something that should be important to other people? Why or why not? (It might be a thing, or an idea, or an event—or anything else that is important to you).

_____

_____

_____

_____

_____

_____

_____

_____

_____

_____

_____

_____

_____

_____

_____

_____

_____

_____

 **Name**

Power Writing

Look at the topics listed below. Pick one that you can write about. Your teacher will time you for three minutes. During these three minutes you should keep writing—do not stop! Do not worry about spelling or punctuation; just keep writing for the entire time. Any idea about the topic should be written down. If you need more space, continue writing on the back of this page. This is called **power writing.**

Pet	Water	Doctor	Wood
Party	A Trip	Senior Citizen	Car

_____

_____

_____

_____

_____

_____

_____

_____

_____

_____

_____

_____

_____

_____

_____

_____

_____

 **Name**

Imagine . . .

Use your imagination. Imagine that trees and flowers could speak to each other. What would a tree have to say to a flower, and how would a flower reply? Create a conversation between a tree and flower and write it below.

_____

_____

_____

_____

_____

_____

_____

_____

_____

_____

_____

_____

_____

_____

_____

_____

_____

_____

 **Name**

Using Your Verbal/Linguistic Intelligence

You have learned about your word intelligence, or your verbal/linguistic intelligence. Think about times when you have used your word intelligence or times when you think your word intelligence might help you to solve a problem. Write about your thoughts.

Title: _____

_____

_____

_____

_____

_____

_____

_____

_____

_____

_____

_____

_____

_____

_____

_____

_____

 **Name**

What Happened Next?

Jerry's father, Doctor Scarvy, was a scientist. One day, Jerry visited his father in the laboratory.

"What's that machine?" asked Jerry.

"It's a time machine," said Doctor Scarvy. "All I have to do is push this button, and it can take us anywhere in time and space!"

"Wow!" said Jerry. "Let's go!"

Write what happened next.

_____

_____

_____

_____

_____

_____

_____

_____

_____

_____

_____

Logical/Mathematical Intelligence

Table of Contents

Grade Level Suggestions for Activity Sheets

Activity Sheet Title	Page	Grade Level(s)
People and Numbers	86	K
Counters	87	K
A Flower and a Tree	88	K
Counting	89	K–1
A Plane and a Train	90	K–1
Similar Science	91	K–1
Shape Patterns	92	1
Fun with Fruit	93	1–2
Daily Digits	94	1–2
Patterns	95	2
Code Creations	96	2–3
Crazy Code	97	2–3
Brainstorm!	98	2–3
Spelling Categories	99	2–4
Knowing My Numbers	100	2–4
Rankings	101	2–4
Pattern Pursuit	102	3–4
Secret Message	103	3–4
Same and Different 1	104	3–4
Same and Different 2	105	3–4
Categories	106	3–4
Using Logic	107	3–4
Number Intelligence	108	3–4
1 2 3, X Y Z	109	4

Logical/Mathematical Intelligence

Description:

In practice, the logical/mathematical intelligence is most evident when a person has to solve a problem. People often think of this intelligence as being scientifically oriented. Actually, we use the logical/mathematical intelligence when we recognize abstract patterns. It is this intelligence that enables us to count by twos and fives or to do the mental math calculations in a restaurant to figure how much of a tip to leave for a waitress. Recognizing relationships between two seemingly unrelated objects is also a product of the logical/mathematical intelligence. People who make lists, set priorities, or make long-range plans are using their logical/mathematical intelligence.

Students who are strong in the logical/mathematical intelligence area think by reasoning. They enjoy questions, figuring out logical problems, doing calculations, and experimenting. They are effectively taught by being given things to explore and think about, science centers, manipulatives, and by satisfying their curiosities.

Development:

The logical/mathematical intelligence begins during infancy. It starts with babies inspecting the objects with which they come into contact. Through this inspection they recognize cause and effect occurrences; for instance, when the baby is hungry, he/she will often get a bottle. At the age of eighteen months, babies will often begin recognizing that certain objects have similar characteristics. Bottles may have different colors and shapes, but they are all used in similar circumstances. Toys, even though they can be very different, can be categorized as such. As soon as babies are able to talk, they very often are able to quantify low numbers of items (1, 2, 3). They might even be able to count up to ten, but until they are four or five, they do not understand numbers as more than just a poem or chant. At this age, they are able to understand the relationship between the words used to describe a quantity and a number of objects.

Complex mathematical and logical thought patterns have to be taught very sequentially. This intelligence does not peak until adolescence or early adulthood. Higher math functions decline when not used and drop after the age of forty.

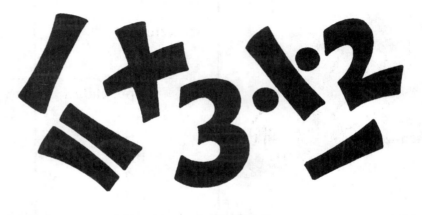

Parents' Letter

Dear Parents,

Our exploration of our intelligences is continuing with numbers and logic. We use numbers every day: to tell how many, what time, how old, and in what order. Our ability to use numbers and logic started long ago when we first recognized cause-effect relationships (when we cried, we were picked up) and characteristics (bottles that fed us were mostly round with a nipple on them). Then we started recognizing many things that could be categorized by characteristics, like toys, books, and people. When we started to talk, we started to count, just with low numbers at first. Our math abilities have continued to develop with opportunities to solve problems and figure things out. There is still so much to find out about numbers and problem solving!

Our time exploring our logical/mathematical intelligence will include doing our regular math, but we will also do so much more. At home you can help to develop this number sense by doing things like the following:

- ✦ Categorize and group random objects by similar characteristics.

- ✦ Follow directions to make something (like a model or a recipe).

- ✦ Play games that require logical thinking or strategy, like *Clue, Monopoly,* or *Battleship.*

- ✦ Brainstorm lists (this develops our number intelligence).

- ✦ Make predictions at different points during a new movie.

- ✦ Create codes with your child and write messages with the codes for others to decipher.

- ✦ Play number games around the table, like how many thumbs there are in all, how many pieces of flatware, how many servings, etc.

The time spent helping your child develop his/her number and logic intelligence will benefit the whole family. Enjoy this quality time together. Its effects will be far reaching! Until next time . . .

Sincerely,

_____

(your child's teacher)

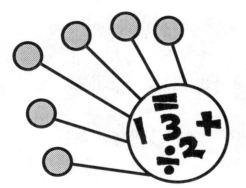

Teaching Students About the Logical/Mathematical Intelligence

Chapter Two

A few weeks after Melanie and Roger found out about being word smart, it was raining again. They had spent quite a lot of time writing stories about different things during the past few weeks, but writing was now becoming a little less exciting. They still liked to write, but they were anxious to find something new to do. Mrs. Burns was still being pretty secretive about the other ways in which they were smart.

"Why can't you give us a hint?" asked Melanie.

"You'll find out soon enough," said Mrs. Burns. This was quite frustrating for the children. They enjoyed trying to think of different ways they were smart, but they just could not quite come up with the right words.

After a little while the rain stopped, and Mrs. Burns agreed to let the children go out as long as they did not get themselves too wet. They were really excited about finally being allowed outside. It was crisp and cool out there. As soon as they got out, Roger noticed some snails again. (Roger really liked to play with bugs and frogs and other things.) He found a great big snail.

"Hey! Look at this one!" he called to Melanie. Melanie did not particularly like the big one, but she found a cute, tiny one that was much more attractive. There were lots of medium-sized snails too.

"I have an idea," said Melanie, "let's do an experiment with the snails."

"What do you mean?" Roger asked.

"Well, you go in and get some paper, a pencil, and a ruler, and we'll pretend we are scientists." Roger was always anxious to play games with Melanie, so he raced in to the house to get the science things she had asked about, even though they did not seem much like science things to him.

When he got back outside Melanie had three snails lined up on the driveway.

"Let's first measure how long the snails are," said Melanie.

They picked up the medium one and put it on the ruler, but it immediately disappeared into its shell.

"How are you going to measure them if they all disappear?" asked Roger.

Teaching Students About the Logical/Mathematical Intelligence

(cont.)

"We'll have to measure them with the ruler next to them instead of under them," Melanie decided. So they measured all of the snails, and Melanie told Roger what numbers to write down. The next thing they decided to do was figure out which ones could travel from one crack on their driveway to the next crack. So they lined the three snails up on one crack, and Melanie told Roger to write down some numbers that told what time they started moving. It took a little while for the snails to start moving, but they finally did.

"How do you know they all want to go to the other crack?" asked Roger. Melanie did not know but said they would just have to keep turning them in the right direction if they turned too much. It was taking quite a long time, and the big snail kept going off to the side. Finally, Roger got bored and suggested that the race end at an earlier crack. Melanie agreed. She did not really like the slimy trail the snails left, anyway. The medium snail reached the crack first. Melanie looked at her watch, and Roger wrote down the time. The big snail reached the crack next (even after he had turned off the course several times). Roger wrote more numbers down.

And then the littlest snail reached the crack. Roger wrote down the final time.

While the snails were racing, Roger had started picking up other snails around the yard.

When he had quite a collection, he started sorting them by size. There were not any quite as small as Melanie's snail, but there were small ones, medium ones, and big ones. He counted 34 snails in all. Most of them were medium ones. He wrote down how many snails were in each size group.

After they had played outside a little while longer, it started drizzling and then raining harder, and Mrs. Burns put her head out the door and called for them to come back inside.

When they were inside, Melanie said that they should record their information. They got some paper and crayons. Melanie drew a graph to record how long each snail took to get from one crack to another. She had forgotten to measure how far apart the cracks were, so she looked out of the window and guessed how far they were. She asked Roger and Mrs. Burns to guess too. Their guesses were all pretty close, so she wrote her number down.

Teaching Students About the Logical/Mathematical Intelligence

(cont.)

Roger made a chart too. On his chart he drew a big circle and divided it into three parts. In each part he drew how many snails there were in each size group. In all, there were 34 snails on his paper.

Mrs. Burns came to see what they were doing. "Hmm," she said. "So you've discovered another way of being smart!"

"No," said Melanie. "We were just pretending to be scientists."

"Exactly," said Roger. They explained what their charts meant.

"So you can see that you are number smart!" said Mrs. Burns. Melanie and Roger looked at each other with big eyes.

"You mean we're word smart *and* number smart?"

"That's right," said Mrs. Burns. "And you still have five to go!" This was great news. Now they could be science journalists. They could figure out all kinds of math and science things and then write about them!

"Hey, but anyone can count snails and stuff," said Roger.

"That's right," said Mrs. Burns, "everyone can be number smart."

At dinner that night Mrs. Burns told Mr. Burns that the children had discovered their logical/mathematical intelligence. Those words were too big for the kids to be bothered with. They were imagining things that they could do with their word and number intelligences the next day. They also could not help but wonder what those other five ways of being smart were. That would have to wait for another rainy day.

Children's Definition:

Being *number smart* means that you can think and solve problems, recognize patterns, put things in order, and do experiments. Anytime you use numbers, solve puzzles, and do scientific things (like planting a seed and learning about the universe around you), you are using your *number intelligence.* Everyone is number intelligent!

Activity:

Ask your classmates about the things they brought in their lunch. Draw a chart or a graph that shows what people have.

Other activities can be found under "Lesson Planning Activities" (page 71) and "Logical/Mathematical Activities Across the Grade Levels" (page 72).

Lesson Planning Activities

The following is a list of activities that you can use when creating a logical/mathematical lesson or when you plan to strengthen this intelligence. Use these activities in combination with those listed under other intelligences to develop a well-rounded curriculum.

- Analyzing
- Abstract Symbols
- Calculations
- Categorizing
- Classifying
- Compare and Contrast
- Critical Thinking
- Deciphering Codes
- Experimentation
- Forcing Relationships
- Formulas
- Graphic Organizers
- Logic Games
- Numbers

- Outlining
- Patterns
- Problem Solving
- Rational Thinking
- Reasoning
- Scientific Thinking
- Sequencing
- Statistics
- Syllogisms (If..., then....)
- Synthesis
- Time Lines
- Venn Diagrams
- Writing Problems

Logical/Mathematical Activities Across the Grade Levels

Mathematics Their Way:

Math Their Way (see bibliography, page 301) works perfectly in conjunction with the multiple intelligence curriculum for the kindergarten and first grades. The pattern identification, sequencing, and hands-on activities are all wonderful logical/mathematical activities. Many early childhood educators are already familiar with this program.

Provide students with a collection of random objects. Ask them to divide these objects into categories. These categories should be student generated. Once the items are classified, ask the students to explain how and why they grouped the objects in the ways in which they did. Model this activity by randomly selecting twelve objects from around the classroom. Have students suggest ways that some of the items might be the same. Guide them to categorize all of the items with a logical explanation.

Grades K–2: For younger students you might want to make the task more manageable by careful object selection. Do not let the objects be too random. Let them fall into two or three pretty obvious categories that students will recognize.

Grades 3 and 4: After students have had practice with this activity, you might decide how many categories there need to be in order to make the task more challenging. Extend the activity by asking the students to use the same objects and classify them differently.

Use the bulletin board idea on the top of page 80 to provide classwide participation in classifying objects.

Step by Step:

Activities that require students to follow step-by-step instructions to complete the project help to develop their problem-solving strategies in a systematic manner.

Priorities:

Helping students to recognize the importance of prioritizing encourages them to develop a lifelong habit and involves their ability to sequence things that are important to them.

Logical Thinking:

Developing your students' abilities to use higher-order thinking helps them solve their own problems. Exercises in If . . . , then . . . . circumstances (cause and effect) work well in these situations.

Number Sense:

Recognizing numbers all around us and pointing them out to students helps them to acknowledge our use of and dependence on this intelligence area. We see numbers in stores (prices), on roads (speed limits and road names), in addresses, on the calendar, etc.

Accessing Logical/Mathematical Intelligence Through Verbal/Linguistic Intelligence

Literature:

There are many books that could be listed here. Counting, logic, categorization, puzzles, problem solving, and experiment books are the types of books to be used to access the logical/mathematical intelligence through the verbal/linguistic intelligence.

All in a Day, by Mitsumasa Anno and Others: Fern Hollow, Random House, 1985

Anno's Counting House, by Mitsumasa Anno: HarpC, 1992

Anno's Mysterious Multiplying Jar, by Masaichiro and Mitsumasa Anno: Philomel, 1983

The Completed Hickory Dickory Dock, by Jim Aylesworth: Aladdin, 1994

Fraction Action, by Loreen Leedy: Holiday, 1994

How Much Is a Million?, by David M. Schwartz: Mulberry, 1994

The I Hate Mathematics! Book, by Marilyn Burns: Little, 1975

Math for Smarty Pants, by Marilyn Burns: Little, 1982

One Crow: A Counting Rhyme, by Jim Aylesworth: Trophy, 1991

One Was Johnny: A Counting Book, by Maurice Sendak: Trophy, 1991

Science Games and Puzzles, by Laurence B. White, Jr.: Lipp Jr., 1979

When Sheep Cannot Sleep, by Satoshi Kitamura: FS & G, 1988

You Be the Jury, by Marvin Miller: Scholastic, 1992

Quantity Sequencing:

Make a pile of books available to the students. Ask them to put the books in order from the book with the most pages to the book with the fewest pages (or vice versa).

Directions:

Logical/mathematical students are good at solving problems. Making a transfer between language and calculations might be a challenge for some. Ask the students to solve problems by following verbal directions.

Kindergarten and first grade students might use blocks or other manipulatives to build verbally specified structures. ("Place a blue block on the table. Put a yellow one next to it on the side of the window. Balance another blue block on top of both of these blocks so that you make a little tunnel," etc.)

Second, third, and fourth grade students can follow simple math calculation instructions.

$$2 + 4 - 3 + 5 + 2 - 4 - 5 = ? \ (1)$$

Accessing Logical/Mathematical Intelligence Through Verbal/Linguistic Intelligence *(cont.)*

Word Classification:

Have students classify a list of words or pictures by types of words (words you can do, words you can touch, words that describe/explain, etc.). This activity can be done orally with younger students or in written form (perhaps a class chart) with older ones.

Compare and Contrast:

Ask the students to do verbal comparisons (written or oral) in various categories. Illustrate this activity by bringing in two stuffed animals. Talk about the ways these animals are alike and different.

Other compare and contrast topic examples include:

"How are you and your friend alike?"
"How are you and your friend different?"

"How is a crayon like a pencil?"
"How is a crayon different from a pencil?"

"How is a bus like a car?"
"How is a bus different from a car?"

"How is a teacher like a mom?"
"How is a teacher different from a mom?"

"How is a bird like a squirrel?"
"How is a bird different from a squirrel?"

"How is a pelican like an eagle?"
"How is a pelican different from an eagle?"

Extension:

Compare two books that have been read in the classroom.

Compare two characters within the same book. (Goldilocks and Mama Bear)

Compare characters with similar roles from two different books. (Cinderella and Snow White)

Accessing Logical/Mathematical Intelligence Through Verbal/Linguistic Intelligence *(cont.)*

Cause and Effect:

Grades K–1: Cause and effect is not a difficult concept for young students to understand. It is a little more difficult for them to verbalize it, however. For these students, short, simple verbal lessons are appropriate. Find examples of cause and effect in daily life, such as in books that you read and in classroom management situations. Point these out during the end-of-the-day ritual or during a discussion/sharing period. After a few examples, students will be able to identify cause and effect without prompting. Examples of cause and effect:

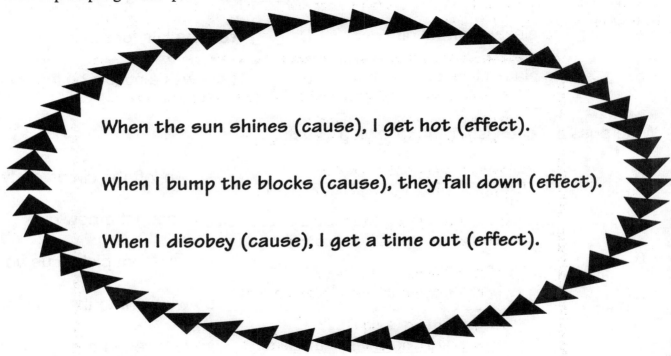

When the sun shines (cause), I get hot (effect).

When I bump the blocks (cause), they fall down (effect).

When I disobey (cause), I get a time out (effect).

Grades 2–4: Cause and effect can be approached a little more formally with older students. Let the students know that sometimes when something happens, it causes something else to happen. For example, when you turn on the faucet, that will cause water to come out. Turning on the faucet is the cause, and water coming out is the effect (see example activity sheet on page 76).

Cause and Effect

Name_____

Match each cause with its most likely effect.

1. ____ Bob stuck a pin in the balloon.   A. ____ We could not see a thing.

2. ____ Traci spilled her milk.   B. ____ The policeman wrote out a ticket.

3. ____ My mom drove too fast.   C. ____ We heard a big pop.

4. ____ The electricity went out.   D. ____ We were late for school.

5. ____ The alarm clock did not ring.   E. ____ There was a puddle on the floor.

Write possible causes for the following effects.

6. _____ so we left the circus early.

7. _____ so I bought a new one.

8. _____ so my mom picked us up.

9. _____ so we went to the mall.

10. _____ so I stayed in bed.

Write possible effects for the following causes.

11. My grandma was not feeling well _____

12. I did not do my homework_____

13. My brother got a yard job _____

14. My sister is too little_____

15. I do not like broccoli _____

Accessing Logical/Mathematical Intelligence Through Visual/Spatial Intelligence

Manipulatives:

Although manipulatives, by definition, fit into the bodily/kinesthetic intelligence area, visual/spatial students also benefit from them. These students can see that math functions that are being done on paper are actual representations of the manipulation and quantifying of objects. Manipulatives should be used with students in all grades.

Picture Classification:

Grades K–2: Give students pictures of animals to color and cut out. Have them glue the pictures by category on a sheet of paper labeled with categories (i.e., large and small, furry and feathered, etc.).

Grades 3–4: Direct students to cut pictures out of magazines. Do not be too specific on what pictures to cut. Let them find pictures that appeal to them personally. Next, ask the students to divide their pictures into categories. These categories can be created by the students or can be teacher directed. Ask the students to paste their pictures onto a sheet of butcher paper, organized in their various categories.

Picture Puzzlers:

Help students to solve puzzles by using visual clues. Spend time explaining (especially to younger students) that there are ways to make putting together puzzles more efficient. Tell them to look for certain characteristics on puzzle pieces instead of trying to make random matches.

Patterns:

A pattern is a group of things or designs that repeat. Give students an example of what a pattern is by drawing several on the board. Give examples of series that are not patterns by drawing them on the board, as well. Have students explain why these are not patterns. To extend this lesson, there are several grade-appropriate pattern activity sheets in the "Logical/Mathematical Activity Sheets" section.

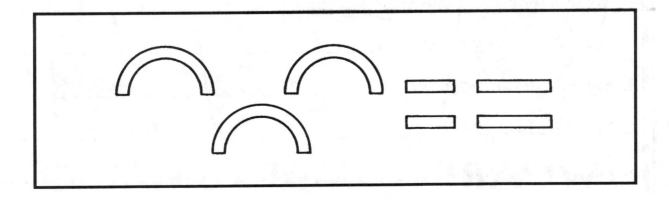

Accessing Logical/Mathematical Intelligence Through Visual/Spatial Intelligence *(cont)*

Displays:

Visual/spatial students like to see the products that are the results of their work.

Displays might include computer programs or printouts, math papers, graphs, charts, comparisons, etc.

Use the bulletin board ideas on the pages that follow for other logical/mathematical displays. Bulletin boards that you have used in the past to teach math or logical thinking can be used in this area, as well. Check your existing resources for many more ideas.

Accessing Logical/Mathematical Intelligence Through Visual/Spatial Intelligence *(cont)*

Cut out pairs of fish from wallpaper sample books or color the fish with identical colors and patterns. Stick one of the pair on the board and the other in the basket. Students can practice pairing them by color and pattern. Be sure to use a board that is low enough for your students to reach. Also, use something besides pins to hold up the fish (i.e., double-sided tape, Velcro squares, paper pockets).

How Many?

Print numbers on the bulletin board. Glue a counted number of small objects (beans, paper clips, candies, etc.) to note cards. Punch a hole in the top of each card. Place the cards with different numbers of objects in the pocket. There can be more than one card per number. Students can hook the cards on the tacks under the appropriate numbers.

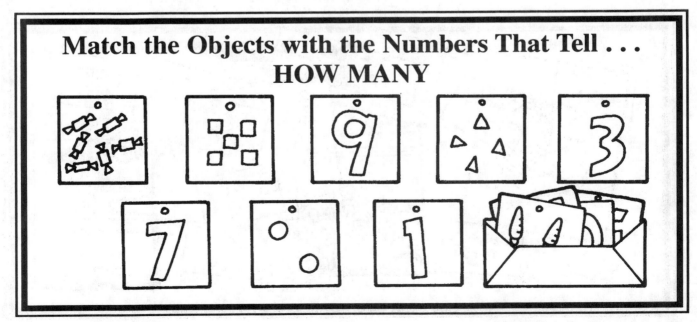

Accessing Logical/Mathematical Intelligence Through Visual/Spatial Intelligence *(cont)*

Types of Cars

Use differently colored construction paper to create separate sections on your bulletin board. Label each section according to the items your class will be classifying. They can either tack, staple, or paste the pictures/objects into the category boxes where they best fit. The example below is based on types of cars with categories such as sports cars, trucks, and station wagons.

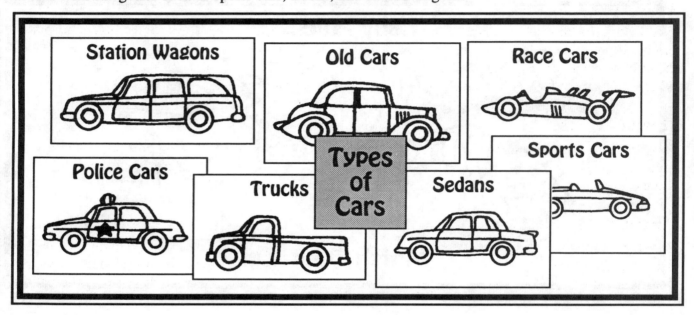

Guess How Many

Attach a plastic zipper bag filled with small objects (candies, beans, pennies, pencils, etc.) to the board. Ask students to estimate how many objects are in the bag. Put estimates on note cards and attach them to the board. At the end of the week put two winners' names (pick two of the closest estimates) on the board. This bulletin board can be used again and again with new sets of objects each week.

Accessing Logical/Mathematical Intelligence Through Bodily/Kinesthetic Intelligence

Field Trips:

Bodily/kinesthetic students learn through moving and touching. Use the list of logical/mathematical oriented careers (listed on page 84) to find places in your community where your students can experience hands-on learning. An example might be a trip to a computer-related operation or a place where someone has to work with changing money (grocery store cashier, bank, post office, etc.)

Human Graph:

Have students create human graphs by lining up in groups by eye colors, lunch contents, clothing, favorite TV shows, etc. Follow up the body graph with a classroom graph where you show how a representation of the people in the graph can be put on paper (visual/spatial extension).

Pattern Games:

Develop number patterns and let students embody the patterns by choosing an action to go with each part. Let them enact the pattern and predict what will come next. Some classroom calendars have repeating patterns in the graphics behind numbers. For example, September might have an alternating pattern between an apple and a book. Let the apple be a clap or jump and the book be a finger snap or a crouch. Develop more complex patterns as time goes by. Students might come up with their own patterns and actions to share with the class.

Body Numbers:

Let students form numbers, using their bodies. A one might be a person standing up straight. A nine would be a person standing with his or her right hand on his or her hip. Some numbers might need more than one body to form. Have students work together to form the numbers. Add new dimensions by having groups of students embody triple digit numbers. Let the rest of the class guess what number each group forms.

Manipulatives:

Hands-on activities help the bodily/kinesthetic student learn in a more concrete manner. Using anything from beans to bodies as counters will help these students to grasp math concepts more easily.

Accessing Logical/Mathematical Intelligence Through Musical/Rhythmic Intelligence

Background Music:

Many teachers already use background classical music during learning periods. This is a great way to help musical students feel at ease while doing something that might not come easily to them. Music that works especially well are selections that have a steady forward movement, like the "Pachelbel Canon." Extend music into the curriculum, however. Try some of the following activities.

Musical Math Facts:

Students can learn counting and other various functions of math easily when they are put to music.

Grades K–1: Fingerplays and chants that deal with counting, patterns, sequence, etc., work well to access the logical/mathematical intelligence through music and rhythm.

Grades 2–4: There are many commercially produced recordings of math facts put to music. Multiplication raps are very popular with students in the higher grades (grades 3 and 4).

Encourage students to develop their own tunes or chants for concepts with which they are having a difficult time. Or, cooperatively develop some classwide learning tools (Interpersonal extension).

Musical Math:

Assign a different sound to various math functions. Let students perform their math problems. For instance, plus (+) might be a clap; equal (=) might be a finger snap. Doing an addition activity repetitively in this manner will help the students remember their facts. Let the students choose their own sounds for the various functions.

Musical Clues:

When students are working on solving a problem, use a selection of music to let them know, by volume signals, whether they are on target or missing the point. The closer they get to solving the problem, the louder the music gets. Use this with individual students or a whole class working on a single problem. The greater the number of students who show they have the correct answer, the louder the music becomes.

Pattern Recognition:

Students who are strong in the musical/rhythmic intelligence will have less trouble recognizing patterns in a musical context. Have them create their own patterns, using musical notes or symbols.

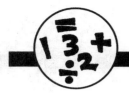

Accessing Logical/Mathematical Intelligence Through Interpersonal Intelligence

Games:

- Strategy games, such as *Clue* and *Monopoly*
- Logical and numerical pattern games, such as *Rummicube*
- Card games, such as *Old Maid, Go Fish,* or *Rook*
- Logical thinking and remembering games, such as *Trivial Pursuit*

Cooperative Math:

Some students enjoy working together. This can take the pressure off of interpersonal students who might have a difficult time with math and logic. It is important for the teacher to establish rules for these students. By definition and nature, interpersonal students love to talk. If they understand that the condition of their being and working together for math time is that they get their work done, they will often have their work completed in a record time so that they can spend free time together, as well.

Any activity in the logical/mathematical section, if done cooperatively by two or more students, would fall under this heading. Many teachers already use formal cooperative learning in their classrooms where students have specific jobs within their groups. David Lazear, in *Seven Pathways of Learning,** outlines specific jobs that can be assigned in a cooperative group.

Checker makes sure each group member understands the content and answers of the lesson.

Scientist helps the group create step-by-step procedures for an assigned task.

Fortuneteller makes predictions about the outcome of the group's work.

Numbers expert checks any math the group performs and the numbers it uses.

Problem solver suggests different ways to deal with the problems the group is to solve.

Detective looks for answer clues as the group works on solving the problem.

Timekeeper watches the clock during timed tasks and adjusts the pace as needed.

Calculator performs math operations for the group.

Thinker helps the group remember, evaluate, and improve its thinking steps.

Patterns expert looks for connections to other subject areas, both in and beyond the classroom.

Peer Evaluation:

Have students trade papers and check each other before they turn in their work to the teacher for final analysis. Set standards by which they do this. The purpose is not to tell each other the answers but to explain how/why they solved a problem in a certain way.

*From *Seven Pathways of Learning,* David Lazear. Tucson, Arizona: Zephyr Press, 1994.

Accessing Logical/Mathematical Intelligence Through Intrapersonal Intelligence

Logic Problem Solving:

Intrapersonal students love to think. They will invariably be good problem solvers. Keep them thinking by having logic-type problems to solve. A good example of these would by syllogisms (If . . . , then . . . .). Offer these as time fillers or reward activities for intrapersonal students.

Behavior Patterns: (Verbal/Linguistic extension)

Have a discussion with your students about behavior patterns. Discuss nonspecific examples that show how various behavior patterns might work positively for them and how others might trip them up. Ask students to think of their own personal behavior and to look for patterns in their behavior that they recognize as working for them and others that work against them.

Biographies:

There are many people who use their intelligence to do great things. Listed below are well-known experts in their fields who would be interesting to study. For younger students, however, it might be more meaningful for them to see and meet someone who uses his or her logical/mathematical intelligence. It is suggested that you use the list of careers to find an individual in your community who uses this intelligence in his/her workplace to come and speak with your class.

- Albert Einstein
- Charles Darwin
- George Washington Carver
- Johannes Kepler
- Thomas Edison
- Marie Curie

Software:

- Math skills tutorial, such as *Math Blaster*
- Computer programming tutors, such as *LOGO*
- Logic games, such as *King's Rule*
- Science programs, such as *Science Tool Kits*
- Critical thinking programs, such as *HOTS—Higher Order Thinking Skills*
- Wings for Learning/Sunburst's *Safari Search*

Careers:

- Accountant
- Actuary
- Auditor
- Banker
- Bookkeeper
- Businessperson
- Computer Analyst
- Computer Programmer
- Doctor
- Economist
- Legal Assistant
- Mathematician
- Purchasing Agent
- Science Researcher
- Science Teacher
- Statistician
- Technician
- Underwriter

Logical/Mathematical Assessment

Logical/Mathematical Processfolio Inclusions:

- Math activity sheets
- Activities that show step-by-step processes
- Science hypotheses that have been tested
- Science experiment reports
- Photographs/videos of science projects (science fair, etc.)
- Evidence of problem-solving abilities (puzzles, brainteasers, etc.)
- Computer generated work
- Graphs, charts, and other statistical analyses by the student
- Codes invented/deciphered by the student
- Checklists for math skills mastery
- Outlines generated by the student
- Evidence of sequencing, categorization, and pattern recognition
- Any product of logical/mathematical lesson planning activities

Evaluation with Logical/Mathematical Intelligence:

- Identify/show understanding of patterns within language.
- Show cause and effect events in history and science.
- Show how to solve . . . .
- Compare and contrast . . . .
- Set up a system by which to organize . . . . (books, papers, recipes, etc.)
- Give a rationale for the rule . . . .
- Solve a mystery.
- Create a time line showing . . . .
- Put the following into categories that you create . . . .
- Make up a story problem that shows . . . .
- Predict what would happen if . . . .
- Conduct a survey of . . . and show results on a chart/graph.
- Justify how you came to the conclusion that . . . .
- Make an outline of . . . .
- Any activity that requires the use of logical thinking or problem solving.

People and Numbers

Circle the pictures of people using numbers.

Counters

Materials: two-sided counters (beans painted on one side work well) and a small paper cup for each student

Example:

Learning the number 6

Put 6 counters in your cup.
Dump your counters on your desk.
Write the sum you see.

2+4=6

1+5=6

Learning the number 4

Learning the number 8

Learning the number 3

Learning the number 5

Learning the number 7

Learning the number 2

A Flower and a Tree

Circle the parts on each picture that are the same.

Counting

Look around the room. There are many things to count. How many windows, students, sweaters, desks, teachers, and bulletin boards are in this room? Count the items in the list below and write the number next to the pictures.

Windows _____

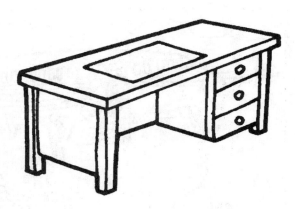

Desks _____

Students _____

Teachers _____

Sweaters _____

GOOD JOB!

Bulletin Boards _____

A Plane and a Train

Look at the two pictures below. Both pictures have parts that are the same and parts that are different. Circle the parts that are the *same.*

Similar Science

Look at the pictures below. Both pictures have parts that are the same and parts that are different. Circle the parts that are the *same.*

Shape Patterns

A pattern is a design or group of things that repeats. Draw a line through the designs that are NOT patterns.

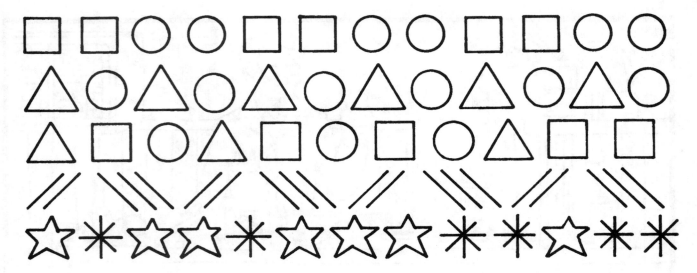

Look for the patterns in the designs below and add three more things to complete them.

Make your own patterns here.

1.

2.

3.

4.

Fun with Fruit

Look at this graph. The graph shows how many people like to eat oranges, how many people like to eat bananas, and how many people like to eat apples.

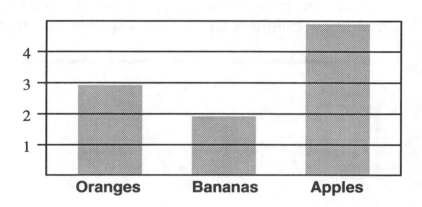

Now look around your class. Notice the different colors of hair that others have. Complete the graph at the bottom of the page to show how many people have the different colors of hair (brown, blonde, red, black).

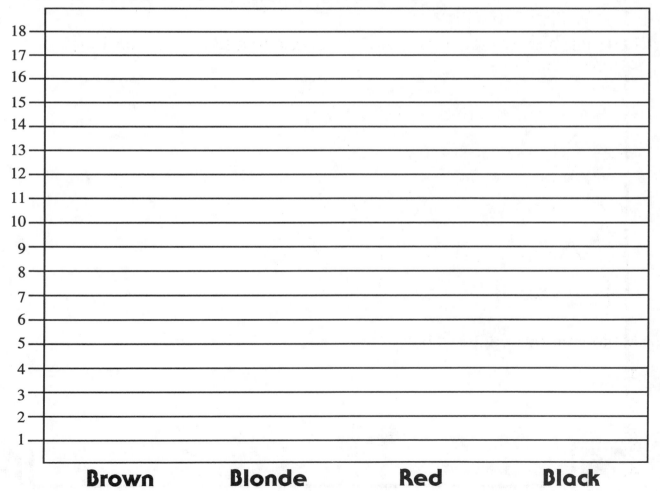

Daily Digits

We use numbers every day. In the box below, draw pictures and write words that show different times and ways we use math.

94

Patterns

A pattern is a group of things that repeats. Draw a line through the designs that do not repeat (the ones that are not patterns).

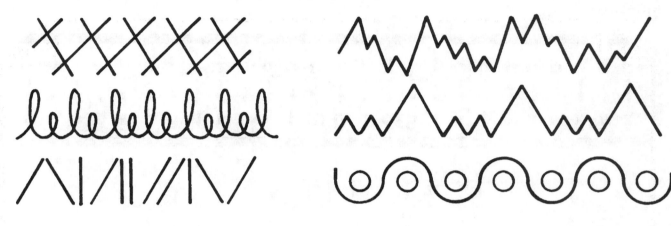

Look for the repeating patterns in each row and add three more things to complete the patterns.

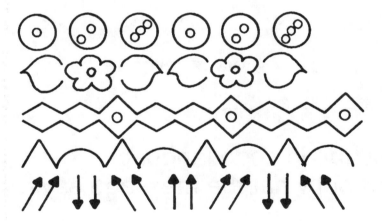

Make your own patterns below.

1.

2.

3.

4.

Code Creations

Look at the coded message below. Use the code key above the message to find out what the code says. Write the answer on the lines below the coded message.

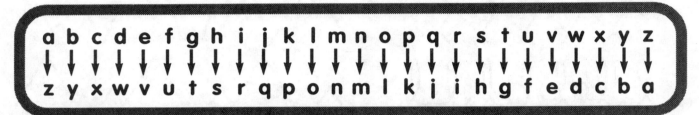

D v   f h v

___ ___   ___ ___ ___

m f n y v i h

___ ___ ___ ___ ___ ___ ___

v e v i b   w z b

___ ___ ___ ___ ___   ___ ___ ___.

Now write your own message in code language. Ask one of your friends to find out what the message says.

Visual/Spatial Assessment

Visual/Spatial Processfolio Inclusions:

- Best drawings, paintings, and sketches
- Photographs/videos of three-dimensional projects
- Evidence of solved visual/spatial puzzles
- Sketches, mind maps, flow charts, etc.
- Murals and montages (or photographs of them)
- Projects that are a result of imagination and visualization
- Demonstrations of manipulations (videos or evidence of)
- Successful map-reading activities
- Activities that illustrate the use of color and shade
- Diagrams of ideas and plans
- Sketches of project development
- Any project that is a product of visual/spatial lesson planning activities

Evaluation with Visual/Spatial Intelligence:

- Create a poster to show . . . .
- Explain the meaning of a picture of . . . .
- Draw a flow chart that shows the sequence of . . . .
- Draw a graphic presentation of . . . .
- Using a map find your way through . . . .
- Create a map of . . . .
- Use manipulatives to demonstrate . . . .
- Create a montage or collage illustrating . . . .
- Illustrate the meaning of a story.
- Design a bulletin board that shows . . . .
- Show your understanding of science by creating . . . .
- Create a scrapbook or video collection documenting . . . .
- Visualize what it would be like if . . . .
- Create a blueprint for . . . .
- Do any activity that requires the use of visualizations or pictures in a response or product.

People and Pictures

Circle the drawings of people using pictures.

At the Park

Look at the two pictures below. They are the same in many ways.
There are ways that they are different. Find how they are different
and circle the different parts on the second picture. Color the top
picture.

 **Name**

Magazine Picture Intelligence

Look for pictures in a magazine that show different people using their picture skills. Cut them out and paste them on this page.

Create a Rainbow

Think of a new shape for a rainbow. Draw your rainbow shape on this page. Then, color your rainbow with new rainbow colors.

Picture It

Think about a book you have read or heard read recently. Draw a picture that shows what the book was about.

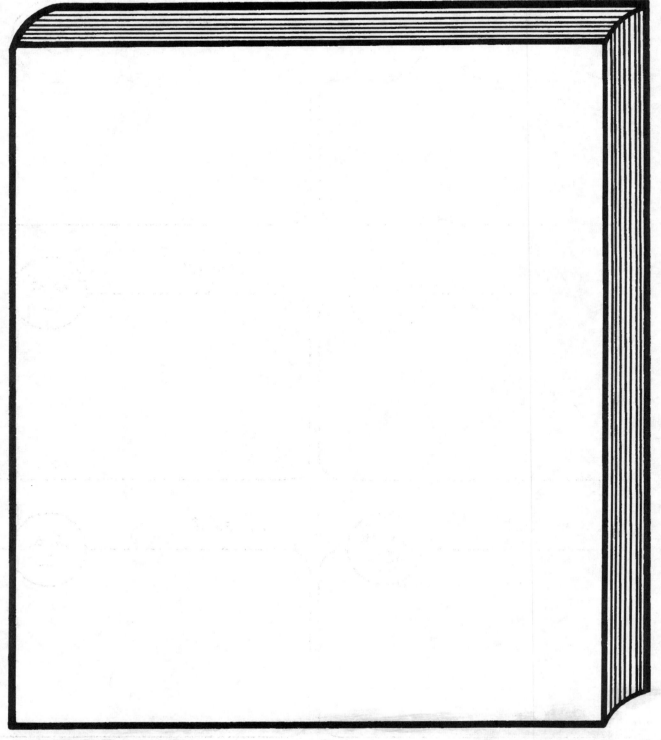

 **Name**

Colorful Feelings

What colors do you see when you are . . .

. . . happy?

. . . angry?

. . . scared?

. . . tired?

. . . excited?

. . . sad?

Picture Intelligence

Draw a picture or several pictures of times when you use your picture intelligence.

Bedroom Map

Draw a map of your bedroom in the space below. Add as many details as you can remember (your bed, dresser, closet, windows, door, etc.).

 **Name**

House Map

Draw a map of your house in the space below. Include as many details as you can remember (bedrooms, kitchen, bathrooms, living room, garage, doors, windows, etc.).

Feelings

Using colors only, color this area to show how you are feeling today.

Scribble Art

In the space below draw a scribble pattern. Look in your scribble pattern and see if you spot any shapes of people, animals, or other objects. Turn your paper to help find an object or objects. Color in the objects and add details to help others see them too.

Name

Draw What You Feel

When people cannot write, they sometimes use pictures to give messages. Think of a picture that will help other people get a message of how you are feeling today. Draw that picture or symbol below.

Smart Advertising

Draw a picture to advertise the seven ways of being smart (word, number, picture, music, body, self, and other).

Tangram

Cut out the tangram at the bottom of this page. Then try to form the diagrams below, using the tangram pieces.

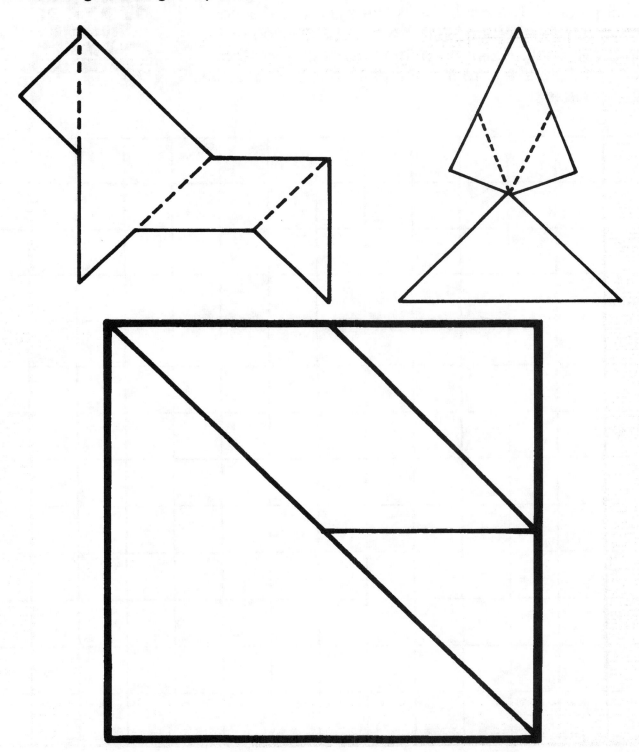

Symmetry

Look at this pattern. This is called a symmetrical pattern. That means that the pattern is balanced on all four sides. The right side is like a mirror reflection of the left. The top half is like a mirror reflection of the bottom half. Color a symmetrical pattern on the grid below. Make sure that the pattern is the same on all four sides.

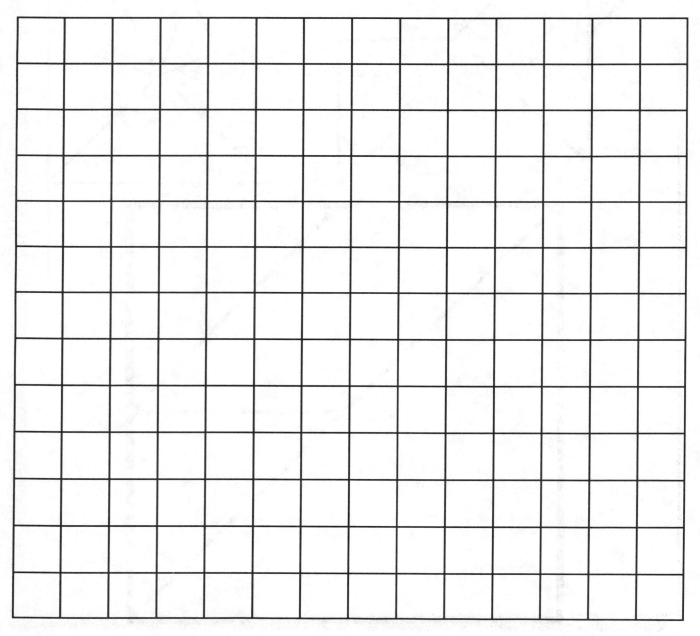

Neighborhood Map

Draw a map of your neighborhood in the space below or use a bigger sheet of paper, if necessary. Include as many details as you can (houses, streets, stores, library, stoplights, etc.).

 **Name**

State Map

Draw a map of your state in the space below or use a bigger sheet of paper, if necessary. Include as many details as you can (cities, roads, bridges, rivers, mountains, train tracks, etc.).

Treasure Hunt

Plan a scavenger hunt for a friend. Draw a map that will help your friend find a treasure. Be sure to show an X to mark the spot of the treasure!

A Different Angle

Draw a picture of an object in the top box. In the bottom box, draw how the same object would look if you were to see it from the top.

 **Name**

Work of Art

Find a poem or quote that is special to you. Rewrite the quote in your most beautiful handwriting. Take your time to do your best. Then, color the border as neatly as you can. Make this sheet a work of art!

Classroom Cartoons

People sometimes get their ideas across by using cartoons. Think of something you recently learned in science or social studies. Draw a cartoon to help get the idea across to someone who might not have learned what you did.

Picture Spelling

Choose four spelling/vocabulary words that you are having difficulty remembering. Look for ways to make a picture for each word to help you remember its spelling and/or meaning. Draw your pictures in the space below See the examples below for ideas on how to do this.

1.

2.

3.

4.

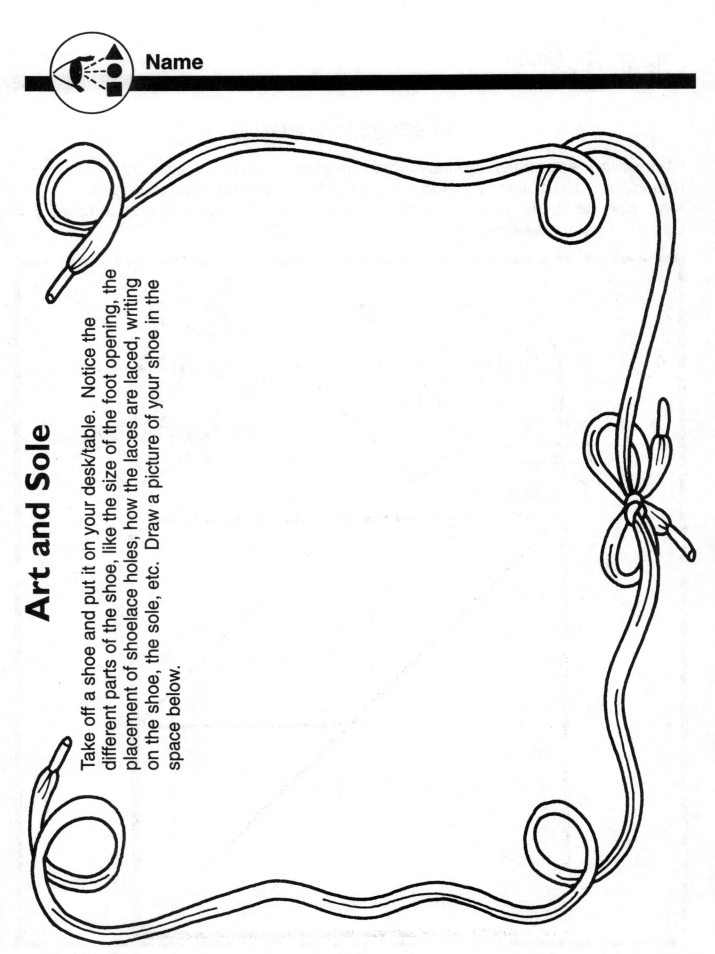

Art and Sole

Take off a shoe and put it on your desk/table. Notice the different parts of the shoe, like the size of the foot opening, the placement of shoelace holes, how the laces are laced, writing on the shoe, the sole, etc. Draw a picture of your shoe in the space below.

Tangram Fun

Cut out the tangram at the bottom of this page. Then try to form the diagrams below, using the tangram pieces.

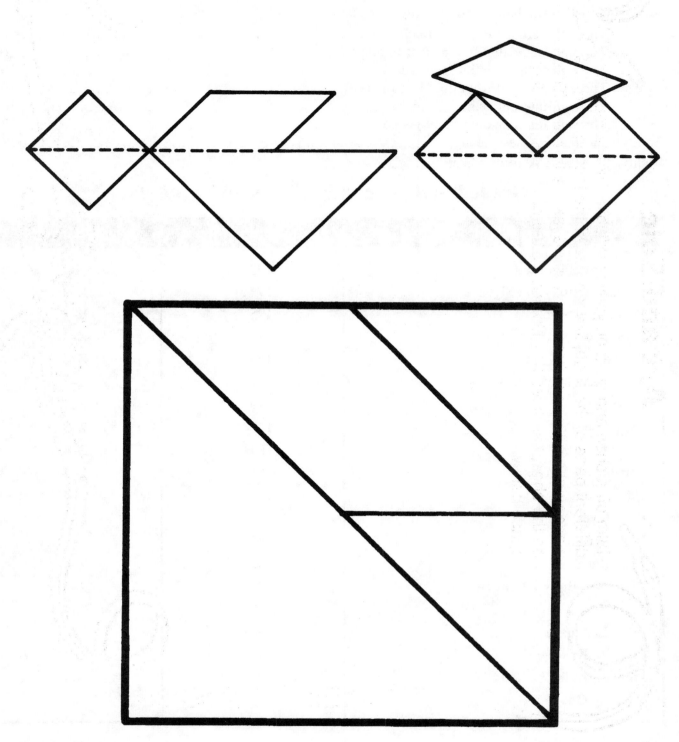

Bodily/Kinesthetic Intelligence

Table of Contents

Grade Level Suggestions for Activity Sheets

Activity Sheet Title	Page	Grade Level(s)
Bodily Intelligence	173	K
Magazine Body Intelligence	174	K–1
Pudding Picture	175	K–1
Serious Cereal	176	K–1
Puzzle Box	177	K–1
Measurement Madness	178	1–2
Cube	179	2
Pasta Spelling	180	2–3
Vocabulary X's	181	2–4
Vocabulary Circles	182	2–4
Quick Copy	183	2–4
Parts Investigation	184	2–4
Body Writing	185	2–4
Drop Race	186	2–4
Using My Body Intelligence	187	2–4
Scarecrow	188	3
Body Language	190	3–4
Exercise Routine	191	3–4
Products of the United States	192	3–4
Working Out	193	4

Bodily/Kinesthetic Intelligence

Description:

The Bodily/Kinesthetic intelligence is at work even when you are not aware of it. Reflex actions such as catching a falling object are a product of the bodily/kinesthetic intelligence. Driving a car is an activity that relies on the bodily/kinesthetic intelligence. A person does not have to consciously think about changing gears, braking, or turning. Once you have learned these skills, you can do it with relatively little thought. Any activity that requires gestures or bodily movement is also one that falls under this intelligence area. Athletes and dancers are professional people who use their bodily/kinesthetic intelligence to a great extent.

Students who are strong in the bodily/kinesthetic intelligence area think through somatic sensations. They enjoy running, moving, building, touching, and gesturing. They learn effectively through role play, drama, sports and physical games, tactile experiences, and hands-on learning.

Development:

The initial presence of bodily/kinesthetic intelligence can be observed as babies look and grasp for different objects around them. It continues as babies are able to pass an object between their two hands and then use various objects for small tasks. From there, the development diverges into two separate pathways: strength and coordination. The development more easily recognizable is the progression of strength and flexibility, and this improves with age. By third grade, students have developed fine-motor coordination. Various bodily/kinesthetic domains are also able to improve but do not really develop until a person has achieved a certain measure of strength and flexibility. Domains are areas such as gymnastics, dance, and tennis.

Parents' Letter

Dear Parents,

We are currently learning how to be smart with our bodies. We use our bodies so much, in fact, it is hard to keep them still. We started developing this intelligence as babies when we would grasp at different objects around us. The development continued as we were able to move things from one hand to another and then used objects to do different things. Developing our coordination is just one area in improving our bodily skills. Treating our bodies properly is important, and learning to do specific activities helps us to improve this intelligence.

We will be doing many activities beyond our regular P.E. and recess activities that will improve our bodily/kinesthetic intelligence. You can help us at home by encouraging and engaging in the following types of activities:

- ✦ Play action games like charades or *Twister.*
- ✦ Express reactions to ideas by using your body (in a gesture or movement).
- ✦ Learn sign language.
- ✦ Do an exercise routine together.
- ✦ Express feelings or emotions through bodily actions.
- ✦ Act out a story together.

I hope you are enjoying learning more about your and your child's different ways of being smart. Remember to keep up with the past intelligences. This development can last a lifetime.

Sincerely,

_____

(your child's teacher)

Teaching Students About the Bodily/Kinesthetic Intelligence

Chapter Four

On a surprisingly sunny Sunday, Melanie and Roger were having fun with all of the neighborhood children, using words, numbers, and pictures to show what they could do. In the late afternoon when the rest of the children had gone home, Melanie and Roger became a little tired of coming up with new ways to use words, numbers, and pictures. They knew they could use them whenever they chose, but they decided to find something new to do.

They had brand new neighbors across the street who did not have any kids. They were still unpacking all of their belongings and were taking advantage of the sunny weather to get the empty boxes out of their house. Melanie and Roger went over to ask if they could have some of the empty boxes to play with. The neighbors were very happy to get rid of the boxes and were glad to let Roger and Melanie play with them. Roger and Melanie took quite a few of the boxes over to their yard. Using the boxes they built a big fort. Then, Melanie built a maze and asked Roger if he could find his way through it. After that, Roger took a turn, and Melanie had to find her way through his maze. They had all kinds of fun using the boxes. They finally built a house with the boxes. It was quite clumsy, though, and it kept falling apart.

"Boy," said Melanie, "I wonder how people keep these things together?"

"We could pretend we're snails and just each have our own little house with us all of the time," Roger suggested.

That sounded like a good idea to Melanie, so they each picked out a box that was just the right size for them to fit inside. It was fun for them to play snail tag. Roger was "it." He had to try to catch Melanie when she was out of her box. She had to carry her box with her wherever she went. If Roger got too close, she could disappear (like snails do) into her shell. Roger finally caught her before she was totally in her box. Then Melanie was "it." That was fun for awhile.

Finally, they decided to pretend to be real snails. "Real snails don't walk on two legs," said Roger. "They have to crawl on their bellies." So they crawled around on their bellies until Mrs. Burns told them that they should not do that anymore to save their clothes from getting more grass stains. Roger decided that snails do not have to worry about grass stains and being hurt on the rough driveway because they have that cool, slimy coating that helps them slide along more easily.

Teaching Students About the Bodily/Kinesthetic Intelligence *(cont.)*

By dinner time, they had become pretty tired of carrying their shells on their backs. They were thankful that they did not have to carry them all over town.

At the dinner table, Mrs. Burns was smiling her mysterious smile again.

"You kids found out you are body smart today!"

"No," said Melanie, "we were tired of practicing being word, number, and picture smart, so we just played other games."

"That's right!" said Mrs. Burns. "The games you played required you to use your bodies. You are body smart."

"You're kidding!" said Roger. "Everybody can run around and play!"

"And everybody can be body smart," said Mrs. Burns.

"Ah, your bodily/kinesthetic intelligence has been discovered," said Mr. Burns. Mr. Burns often used words Melanie and Roger did not understand. But that was okay. They had just discovered their fourth way of being smart. Now they could use words, numbers, pictures, and their bodies! "Only three to go," thought Melanie.

Children's Definition:

Being body smart means that you can use your body to run, jump, walk, and sit. You can also use it to show how you are feeling. Anytime you play a game in which you use your body, go out to recess, or make something using your hands, you are using your bodily intelligence. Everyone is body smart.

Activity:

Pretend you are a snail. What does a snail do? Now pretend you are a rabbit. What does a rabbit do? How about a duck? An elephant? A cow?

Other activities can be found under "Lesson Planning Activities" (page 159) and "Bodily/Kinesthetic Activities Across the Grade Levels" (pages 160 and 161).

Lesson Planning Activities

The following is a list of activities that you can use when creating a bodily/kinesthetic lesson or when you plan to strengthen this intelligence. Use these activities in combination with those listed under other intelligences to develop a well-rounded curriculum.

- Acting

- Body Answers

- Body Language

- Body Maps

- Body Sculpture

- Charades

- Classroom Theater

- Collections

- Dancing

- Demonstrations

- Dramatization

- Exercise

- Experiment

- Field Trips

- Folk and Creative Dance

- Gymnastics

- Hands-on Thinking (clay, manipulatives)

- Human Graph

- Human Tableaux

- Impersonation

- Improvisation

- Inventing

- Martial Arts

- Mime

- Movement

- Physical Education

- Puppetry

- Role Playing

- Skill Demonstration

- Sports Games

- Visiting

Bodily/Kinesthetic Activities Across the Grade Levels

Any activity which allows students to be up and moving or touching will help them to learn materials more effectively. Luckily, most of the primary curriculum caters to this need fairly well. Be sure that students are able to manipulate objects across the curriculum, not only in isolated parts of their school days.

Field Trips:

Bodily/kinesthetic learners absorb the most by doing and feeling. Many community members are happy to enrich the learning of students by providing hands-on opportunities. Use the list of careers at the end of this section and your phone book to find places in your community that will best meet your and your students' needs.

Simulations and Role Plays:

Simulations and role play are excellent bodily/kinesthetic activities. These activities require students to take what they have learned and apply it to real-life situations. These activities do not always need to be teacher directed. After learning about a certain topic, have the students divide into groups and develop their own simulations to do by themselves or in front of the class. Simulations and role plays work well for students across the grade levels.

Bodily Answers:

Teachers always use this technique in the form of "Raise your hand if you . . . ." Add variations to your repertoire to keep the attention of the bodily/kinesthetic learners. Variation ideas include these:

"If you can tell me two (or more) things about what we just learned, stand on one foot" (students will be stretching their brains to come up with two things just so they can stand on one foot).

"When you have the answer and you *know* it's right, smile; if you *think* it's right but aren't positive, show "thought" on your face" (this might come after practicing various facial expressions so students are familiar with their ability to communicate with their expressions).

Instead of taking a vote by a show of hands, have students in favor of one option face the back of the room. Those in favor of the different option can face the front. This might take time and practice to help them deal with the curiosity factor during face count (when they turn around to see which way their friends are facing, they might get counted for the opposite option). This is a great exercise in self-control. They will get used to the idea soon.

Physical Exercise:

Physical exercise is probably the one bodily/kinesthetic activity that continues in schools after the lower grades are completed. It is important. Students need the stimulation that exercise gives. Help your students develop a good attitude toward exercise. Give time between heavy subject matter for stretching and getting the blood and oxygen moving.

Bodily/Kinesthetic Activities Across the Grade Levels *(cont.)*

Play Dough or Clay:

The power of play dough or clay might often be overlooked. Many classrooms, especially in the lower grades, have this material available, but it is often used during playtime only. Spread the use across the curriculum. Have students write their vocabulary/spelling words using the dough. Ask them to sculpt something that deals with the topic of discussion. Have them express feelings through clay faces. Ask them to create book characters from their dough. Have them use dough for math manipulatives. Then they can write the math problems using the dough. Have several students create scenes to show a sequence in a story. (Ask each student to take one scene and then put all of the scenes in sequential order.) The options are limitless.

Have each student bring a butter/margarine container (the ones that seal) or a plastic zipper bag from home. Use the recipe below to make a batch or two of dough. Each student can keep his/her own ball of dough fresh in the sealed container for up to two weeks.

Play Dough Recipe

- 3 cups (735 mL) flour
- food coloring (optional)
- ½ cup (125 mL) vegetable oil (or several drops of liquid detergent)
- 1 cup (250 mL) salt
- 1 cup (250 mL) water

Mix flour and salt together in a large bowl. Slowly add water, oil (or detergent), and food coloring. Knead and use the dough immediately or store it in an airtight container for future use.

You might want to preserve some clay projects. To do this, use cornstarch clay.

Cornstarch Clay Recipe

- 1 cup (250 mL) cornstarch
- 1½ cups (375 mL) cold water
- 2 cups (500 mL) salt

Put salt and ⅔ cup (167 mL) water in a pot and bring to a boil. Mix cornstarch in remaining water and stir well. Blend these two mixes together and knead into clay. This clay takes several hours to dry.

To preserve clay projects:

Let students form clay into objects they want to preserve (flat, ornament-type objects work best). Bake the dough at 225° F (107°C) for two hours, turning occasionally to prevent curling. Paint with tempera colors and allow to dry.

Accessing Bodily/Kinesthetic Intelligence Through Verbal/Linguistic Intelligence

Literature:

Books that have action in the story line work well in the bodily/kinesthetic intelligence area. Repetitive language books are also effective when you associate repetitive vocabulary with actions. Reading the book orally and having the students do the actions help them to access their bodily/kinesthetic intelligence through the verbal/linguistic intelligence.

- *Iktomi and the Buzzard,* by Margaret Hillert: Orchard Books, 1994

- *My Hands*, by Aliki: Crowell Jr., 1990

- *Rhythm Road: Poems to Move To*, by Lillian Marrisan: Lothrop, Lee, and Shepard Books, 1988

Models:

Allow students to do various tasks or build models by following written or oral directions. Having these guidelines available to them will assist students who do not feel confident in the bodily/kinesthetic intelligence area.

Communicating Directions:

Ask the students to think of a specific task, such as watering a plant or making peanut butter and jelly sandwiches. Have them write specific directions for an alien to follow so that the alien could complete the task. Younger students can give these directions orally. Older students might write them. Have a sophisticated listener follow the directions precisely to show how specific the directions need to be. (The instruction teller might have forgotten to have the alien remove the peanut butter jar lid, etc).

Sports Reporters:

Let the students enter the world of radio and television reporters. They will report on sports events on the playground. Have them give a blow-by-blow description of what is happening.

Spelling with Pasta:

Set up a table with a bowl of alphabet pasta, glue, graph paper, and a spelling or vocabulary list. Have students spell their words, using the pasta letters and gluing them onto the graph paper for a hands-on spelling activity.

Accessing Bodily/Kinesthetic Intelligence Through Verbal/Linguistic Intelligence *(cont.)*

Book Reports in a Bag:

Instead of *writing* a book report, have students do a report that they can show. This can be done with students at any age. Let each student decorate a paper bag with the title and author, as well as an illustration of something that happened in the book. Then, fill the bag with things that can help tell about the book. For instance, older students might write a short summary of the book on a stiff piece of tagboard that is in the shape of the book. Small objects that relate to the book can be placed in the bag. Key words or pictures that pertain to the book can be cut out of magazines and placed in the bag. Students should be able to report about the objects in their bags. Classmates will randomly draw things out of the bag, and the student will explain why the objects are in there and what they have to do with the book. This activity can be used for reporting on books read at home and act as an advertisement for the books so that other students will want to read them too.

Accessing Bodily/Kinesthetic Intelligence Through Logical/Mathematical Intelligence

Kid Cooks:

Following a recipe to make a simple dish is a great way to access the bodily/kinesthetic intelligence through the logical/mathematical intelligence. The sequence and specific instructions guide students through a positive hands-on experience.

Body Patterns:

After creating or recognizing a pattern in the logical/mathematical intelligence area, have students do bodily actions for each part of the pattern and then do the pattern. One symbol might be a jump; the other, a low crouch or a clap. Being able to predict what action comes next by looking at the pattern will remove the anxiety of using their bodies.

Graph Models:

A variation on drawing a chart or graph to show results of a survey might be to build a chart or graph using blocks or dried food (noodles, beans, etc.) on construction paper. Students will be transferring the logical/mathematical knowledge they already have to the lesser developed bodily/kinesthetic intelligence area.

Bodily Graphs:

An additional variation to the chart/graph idea above is to have the students make a graph using their bodies. For instance, students might divide themselves into groups by how many people there are in their families. Those with four or fewer people in one line, five in another line, and six or more in a third line. Students will then be and see a graphic representation of this particular survey. Advanced students might represent a larger population of people (maybe all the students in the school) by letting their bodies represent more than one person.

Bodily Math:

Practice addition and subtraction with students by the colors they are wearing. For instance, have all of the children wearing blue jeans stand in the front of the class. Add (+) other students wearing white shirts. How many children are there in all? Then subtract (-) all of the children wearing purple shoes. How many children are there now? Continue, using clothing colors, hair color, eye color, etc.

Accessing Bodily/Kinesthetic Intelligence Through Visual/Spatial Intelligence

Visualization:

Grades 2–4: After learning about a particular topic, have students close their eyes and lead them on an imaginary tour of a related activity they will actually be doing. Help them to visualize the process they will be going through, step by step. Describe a beautiful, successful project. Give specific details of how that project was achieved. After they have visualized doing the activity, have them open their eyes and actually do it. Taking the time to go through all of the steps before beginning the activity might help students plan carefully for the steps of the actual activity. If they can see what they should do in their imaginations, they will have an easier time making the connection in real life.

Animated Colors:

Grades K–2: A connection between feelings and colors was made between the visual/spatial and intrapersonal areas. Now guide the students through a colors and actions connection. This might be less intimidating if you use color crayons as puppets. If RED were to act, what would he/she do? What would BLUE do? How about GRAY? Let students show their ideas of what the different crayons would do. Then, put the crayons away and let students each decide on actions for themselves. Pretend you are YELLOW. What would you do? Now you are PURPLE. Show what purple does.

Picture Reporting:

After going on a field trip, help visual/spatial students to access what they did and saw by having them draw a picture to report on the event. The picture, for them, will be like a camera image that will commit their learning to a deeper level. Letting them know of this activity before they leave on the field trip will enable them to take pictures throughout the day and make the same connection without having paper and crayons to actually go through the process. They can make their plans for pictures in their minds.

Edible Art:

With colored chalk draw a rainbow on the board. Discuss its many colors. Then give each student a paper plate with three blobs of colored pudding, icing, cream cheese, or yogurt — one yellow, one blue and one red. Give each student a craft stick and challenge each to make the colors of the rainbow. Later, give each student a graham cracker on which to paint a minirainbow. When it is all done—eat the art!

Accessing Bodily/Kinesthetic Intelligence Through Visual/Spatial Intelligence (cont.)

Displays:

Visual/spatial students like to see evidence of what they can do. Create displays that include their work and encourage them to use their bodies.

See the bulletin board ideas on this page and the next for other bodily/kinesthetic displays. Use the displays from your existing resources to supplement this section.

Our Favorite Games

Tennis	Football	Baseball	Soccer	Basketball

Create a pictograph for the bulletin board. Take a survey of which sport each student prefers and display the results. You might wish to add names to the tags on the graph.

This bulletin board can also be used with other surveys (favorite teams, subjects, foods, activities, etc.).

Accessing Bodily/Kinesthetic Intelligence Through Visual/Spatial Intelligence *(cont.)*

Display different body smart activities on a bulletin board similar to the one above.

Use the bottom bulletin board idea to remind students to cultivate all seven intelligence areas, not just one or two.

Accessing Bodily/Kinesthetic Intelligence Through Musical/Rhythmic Intelligence

Field Trip Songs:

After going on a field trip, spend time with the class processing what they saw and learned. Have the students pick a familiar tune and then create a song about their experiences. There might be songs in your repertoire already that deal with the concepts learned and reinforced on the field trip. These could be sung as well.

Musical Exercise:

This is not a new concept to anybody. Exercise routines have been set to music for a long time now. There are several kid routines set to children's music and available in retail stores. Or, you can have your class develop their own exercise routines to their favorite songs.

Music Models:

A variation on drawing a response to music (musical/rhythmic intelligence) might be to have students build a model as a response to a piece of music. Play a selection of music with which your students may already be familiar. After they have listened to it once, tell them that they will be building models out of colored paper and glue (or another medium you select) which shows what they hear in the music. Let them listen to the selection again. After they have listened to it a second time, give them access to the materials and let them listen to the music while they work. Ask for volunteers to show what they have created as a response to the music, including descriptions and/or explanations (interpersonal and intrapersonal extension).

Musical Instruments:

Children of all ages have made musical instruments out of all types of materials. This is a great musical/rhythmic and bodily/kinesthetic connection. These are several books available that can help generate ideas. One particularly helpful book is *Making Musical Things* by Ann Wiseman (Macmillan Publishing Company). This book includes directions for making a variety of musical instruments from easily obtainable materials such as milk cartons and embroidery hoops.

Accessing Bodily/Kinesthetic Intelligence Through Interpersonal Intelligence

Games:

- Role playing and mime games, such as charades
- Motor coordination and balance games, such as *Twister*, creating human pyramids, or pickup sticks
- Bodily language games such as mirroring a partner's movements or expressing emotions
- Multitracking games, such as jogging in place, snapping your fingers, and blinking all at the same time

Puppet Arms:

Ask students to pair up. One student will stand behind the other with his or her arms in front of the other (front) partner. The partner in front should put his/her arms behind his/her back and may start speaking. At the same time, the person in the back will use his/her arms as if they were the speaker's arms. More exaggerated gestures make funnier routines. Let the students imitate various professions and activities, and sound effects should be included.

Cooperative Models:

Any assignment in which students build models can be done in groups of two or more. Students who do not feel comfortable building or making things might feel less intimidated if they are able to share the task with another person or group of people. These models might be out of paper, clay, blocks, pipe cleaners, paper clips, etc. In his book *Seven Pathways of Learning**, David Lazear outlines tasks for a bodily/kinesthetic cooperative group.

Actor helps the group think of role-playing ideas for acting out parts of a lesson.

Dancer suggests creative physical movements that could be part of the group's report.

Coach helps the group learn physical movement routines to embody what the group learns.

Inventor creates new steps, procedures, and active ways to do old things.

Choreographer helps the group plan its staging of a report or presentation.

Gesture manager suggests body language to communicate group feelings about a lesson.

Athletic coordinator thinks of physical games to play that are related to a lesson or task.

Mimer creates nonverbal ways to show what the group has learned in a lesson activity.

Stage director helps the group practice and perfect an upcoming presentation.

Props manager helps the group find any presentation props it needs.

*From *Seven Pathways of Learning*, David Lazear. Tucson, Arizona: Zephyr Press, 1994.

Accessing Bodily/Kinesthetic Intelligence Through Interpersonal Intelligence *(cont.)*

Table Groups:

Students who ordinarily do not choose to do bodily/kinesthetic activities might be more prone to choose them if a group of their peers are already at work in that area. Jigsaw puzzles provide a good connection. A table for play dough or clay might encourage participation. Blocks and other manipulatives can be used in groups or pairs. Relieve bodily/kinesthetic anxiety by allowing for group work.

Sports Games:

A regular recess activity provides a great bodily/kinesthetic-interpersonal connection. Encourage the participation of all students with reassuring peer participation. Be sure to choose activities that are not competitive, like catching a ball/beanbag (between two or among three students), jumping rope, playing tag, etc.

People Sculpting:

Have students pair up and take turns in each role—one student will be the sculptor; the other, the dough. Have the sculptors mold their clay by carefully bending their partner's arms, legs, waist, etc. The clay is to maintain the position into which it is molded. After a set amount of time (three to five minutes) let the sculptors name their works of art. Allow the sculptor and clay to switch responsibilities and repeat the activity.

Accessing Bodily/Kinesthetic Intelligence Through Intrapersonal Intelligence

Emotions Pantomime:

Ask students to think about how they are feeling at a specific time (present tense). What actions would they use to show that feeling or group of feelings? Give students time to act their emotions. Let them guess what classmates are feeling by the actions being done around them.

Multitracking Activities:

Help your students to develop the ability to do several activities at one time, such as listening to a story and drawing a picture simultaneously. As they develop this ability, move on to three tasks at the same time, like listening to music, cleaning his/her area, and watching for a guest speaker all at once.

Biographies:

There are many people who use their intelligences to do great things. Listed below are well-known experts in their fields who would be interesting subjects to research. For younger students, however, it might be more meaningful for them to see and meet someone who uses his/her bodily/kinesthetic intelligence. It is suggested that you use the list of careers below to find an individual in your community, who uses this intelligence in the workplace, to come and speak to your class.

- Babe Ruth
- Jim Thorpe
- Kristi Yamaguchi
- Mickey Mantle
- Thomas Edison
- Isadora Duncan
- Cincinnatus
- Fabergé
- Wilbur and Orville Wright

Software:

- Hands-on construction kits that interface with computers, such as *LEGO to LOGO*
- Motion-simulation games, such as *Flight Simulator*
- Virtual reality system software, such as *Dactyl Nightmare*
- Eye-hand coordination games, such as *Shufflepuck Cafe*
- Tools that plug into computers, such as *Science Toolkit*

Careers:

- Actor/Actress
- Athlete
- Carpenter
- Choreographer
- Craftsman
- Dancer
- Farmer
- Forest Ranger
- Inventor
- Jeweler
- Mechanic
- Mime
- P.E. Teacher
- Physical Therapist
- Professional Dancer
- Recreational Director

Bodily/Kinesthetic Assessment

Bodily/Kinesthetic Processfolio Inclusions:

- Samples or photographs of projects done
- Video recordings of activity processes
- Sketches and diagrams of projects in progress or completed
- Recordings of dramas and simulations
- Photos of human sculpture or human tableaux
- Physical exercise routine ideas (student generated)
- Inventions or ideas for inventions
- Checklists for skill mastery levels
- Reports of hands-on activities (lab experiments, etc.)
- Observation reports or illustrations, using body and gestures
- Any record or product from bodily/kinesthetic lesson planning activities

Evaluation with Bodily/Kinesthetic Intelligence:

- Using your body, show . . . .
- Illustrate (history/science) through a dramatization.
- Invent something to show . . . .
- Through creative movement demonstrate your understanding of . . . .
- Follow directions to make a . . . .
- Act out how a person feeling . . . might act.
- Do an exercise routine which proves your ability to . . . .
- Show you understand the story character by acting . . . .
- Illustrate results of a survey with a human graph (using classmates).
- Show your understanding of vocabulary words through . . . .
- Use manipulatives to show . . . (math function)
- Do any activity that requires the use of the body in response to a project.

Body Intelligence

Circle the pictures of people using their bodies.

 **Name**

Magazine Body Intelligence

Find pictures in magazines of people using their body intelligence. Cut the pictures out and paste them on this page.

Pudding Picture

Teacher's Note: Mix chocolate or berry pudding as directed on the package. Give each student a sheet of tinfoil with three spoonfuls of pudding on top. Let the students create a pattern on the foil (if finger painting is too messy, you may wish to use tongue depressors to spread the pudding) and then press this activity sheet carefully over the pattern. Lift this paper and then allow it to dry for several hours.

Press this sheet over your pudding pattern carefully and then lift it up. Let your pattern dry before you take it home with you!

Serious Cereal

Teacher's Note: Copy this sheet onto brightly colored paper for the best results. Let students share a cupful of o-shaped cereal. Instruct your students to dab small glue dots on their activity sheets (5–6 at a time) to form a design or allow them to dip the cereal in glue before placing them on the sheets.

Using cereal and glue, carefully make a picture on the cereal box below. Your picture can be an object or just a pattern—it's your choice!

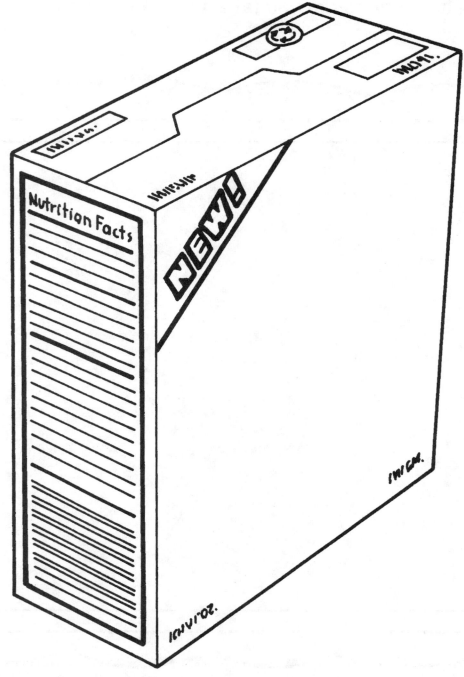

Name

Puzzle Box

To the Teacher: (Enlarge puzzle as needed.) Have students cut out the puzzle pieces, put the pieces in a bag, mix them up, and put the puzzle back together again. If you wish, have students color or make designs on the puzzle pieces before cutting them out.

Measurement Madness

Materials: paper clips, pennies, beans, ruler

Using the items listed above, measure how long each of the following things is.

	paper clips	beans	pennies	inches
your hand				
top of your desk				
seat of your chair				
cover of a reading book				
around a lunch box				
side of this paper				

178

Cube

Decorate the cube with designs or written messages. Cut out the pattern along the solid lines. Fold along the dashed lines and glue the tabs in place to form a cube. Allow the glue to dry. Tape string or yarn to one side of the cube and hang it up for display.

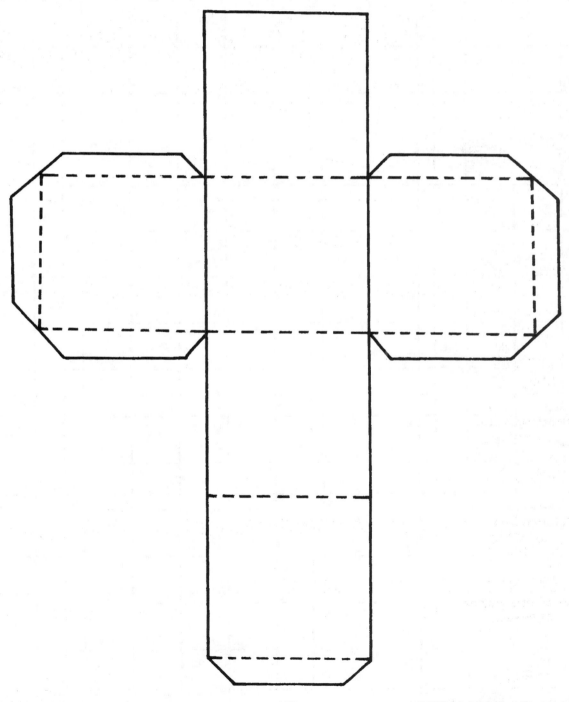

Pasta Spelling

Using pasta letters and glue, paste your spelling words onto this activity sheet. Be sure to put only one letter in each square. See the example pictured below.

P	A	S	T	A								

Vocabulary X's

Write your vocabulary or spelling words in large letters on the lines below. Then go back over each letter with tiny x's. Try to make all the x's the same size. Look at the example below and finish marking the x's on the last letters for practice.

BODY SMART

_____   _____

_____   _____

_____   _____

_____   _____

_____   _____

_____   _____

_____   _____

_____   _____

_____   _____

Name

Vocabulary Circles

Write your vocabulary or spelling words in big letters on the lines below. Go back over each letter with tiny circles. Try to make the circles all the same size. See the example below and finish putting the circles on the last letters for practice.

BODY SMART

_____   _____

_____   _____

_____   _____

_____   _____

_____   _____

_____   _____

_____   _____

_____   _____

_____   _____

 **Name**

Quick Copy

Look at the patterns started below. Try to complete the patterns across each
line as *quickly* and as *neatly* as you can.

Parts Investigation

There are many things around us that have several parts. Take time to explore the parts. Think about what each part is needed for. Use this activity sheet to guide you.

Take apart a pen. Draw the separate parts here:

What does each part do? Why are they necessary?

_____

_____

_____

Take apart a flower. Draw the separate parts here:

Think about what each part does. Keep exploring and thinking!

Body Writing

You already know how to write. Now try writing in ways you might not have tried before.

Write your name again here: _____

Use your other hand to write your name here:_____

Put your pencil in your mouth and try writing your name again here:

_____

Take off your shoes and socks. Put your pencil between your toes and write your name here:

_____

Now use your other foot:

_____

Which was the hardest for you to use? _____

Which was the easiest? _____

Besides writing, what other everyday activities could you try to do using these bodily parts?

_____

_____

_____

Drop Race

Cover this page with a sheet of wax paper. Fold the wax paper over to the back and Scotch tape it in place.

Using your finger, place a medium-size drop of water (from a faucet or a cup of water) into the starting circle.

Guide the drop of water through the maze by moving the sheet of paper around. After practicing for a few minutes, challenge a classmate to a water-drop race. Take turns seeing who can get the drop through the entire race course without going out of the lines and without dropping the drop. Have fun!

Teacher's Note: This activity also works well when the activity sheets have been laminated. If you do choose to laminate, save a class set to use year after year.

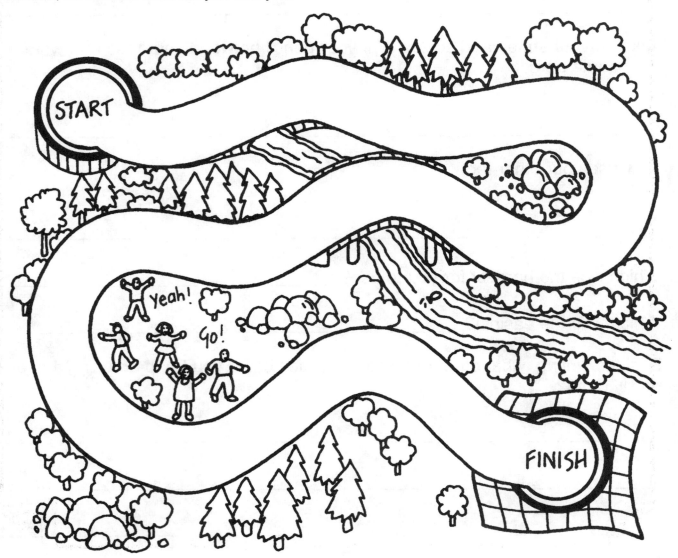

Using My Body Intelligence

There are many things we do that require us to use our body intelligence. Think about the ways you use this intelligence. Draw or cut and paste pictures that show the different ways we use the bodily/kinesthetic intelligence.

Scarecrow

Use the following directions to make your own scarecrow.
1. Use the patterns to cut out the pieces from different colors of construction paper.
2. Glue the head onto the collar.
3. Glue the hat onto the head.
4. Glue the two eye parts of each eye together and then attach the eyes onto the head.
5. Glue the teeth onto the mouth and the cheeks onto the corners of the mouth.
6. Glue the mouth and the nose onto the head.
7. Use scraps of paper to make patches for the collar and hat and scraps of yarn for a bow tie and hair.

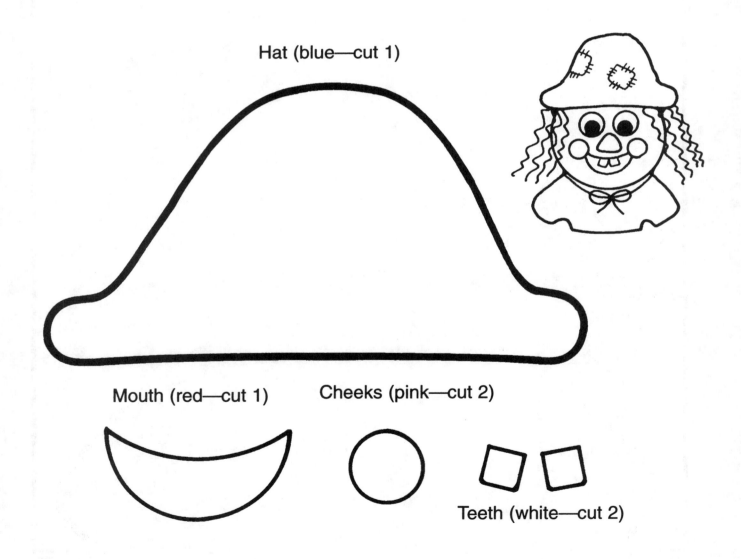

Hat (blue—cut 1)

Mouth (red—cut 1)   Cheeks (pink—cut 2)

Teeth (white—cut 2)

Scarecrow *(cont.)*

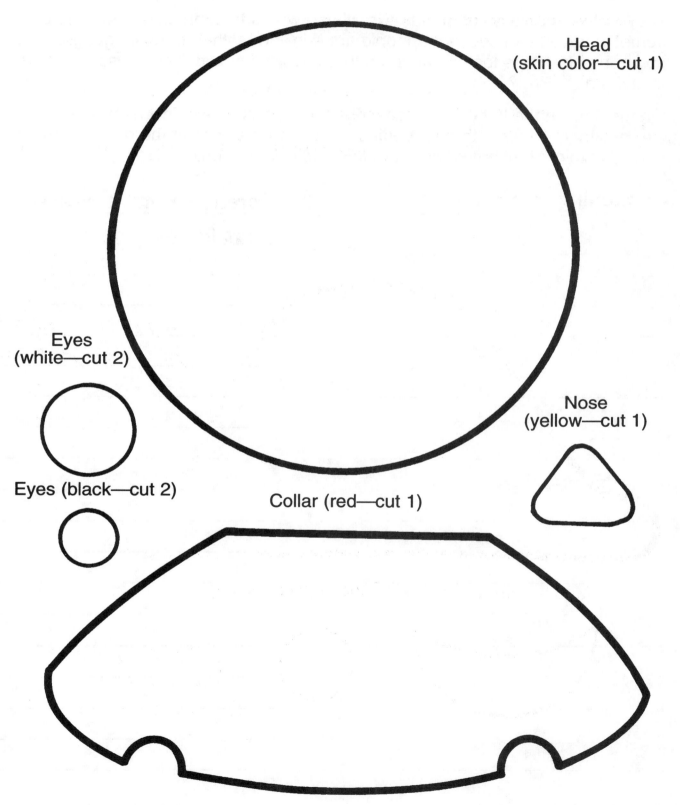

Head
(skin color—cut 1)

Eyes
(white—cut 2)

Nose
(yellow—cut 1)

Eyes (black—cut 2)

Collar (red—cut 1)

Name

Body Language

Look at the people around you. We all use words to express ourselves, but sometimes you can see what people are thinking by their body language. If someone else were looking at you right now, what would they guess you were thinking or feeling?

On the lines in the left column, describe the different ways in which people express themselves with their bodies. Then, on the lines in the right column, tell what you think they are saying with this bodily language.

Slouching in a chair

Bored or not interested in what is going on

_____

_____

_____

_____

_____

_____

_____

Exercise Routine

Many people use an exercise routine to keep healthy. Some people develop exercise routines as their jobs. For example, aerobics instructors, gymnasts, football players, and dancers all have very specific routines.

Develop your own exercise routine here. You can choose what style to use—straight exercise (as in P.E.), a gymnastic routine (for yourself or for a group), or a dance routine—it's your choice. After you have thought through your routine and practiced it, write it down or draw (diagram) the process. Be ready to share your exercise routine with your classmates.

Exercise Sequence

_____
_____
_____
_____
_____
_____
_____
_____
_____
_____
_____
_____
_____
_____
_____
_____

Diagram of Routine

Products of the United States

The things around us come from many different places. Look inside books. Where are they printed? Where are the crackers in your lunch made? Find out which area in the United States produces the most things in your life by doing a survey of the labels around you. When you find something from a particular state, write that object inside the state (or next to the state if it cannot fit). Keep working on your survey during your spare time until you have at least 50 objects written down. You might check out some labels at home too, especially on the groceries.

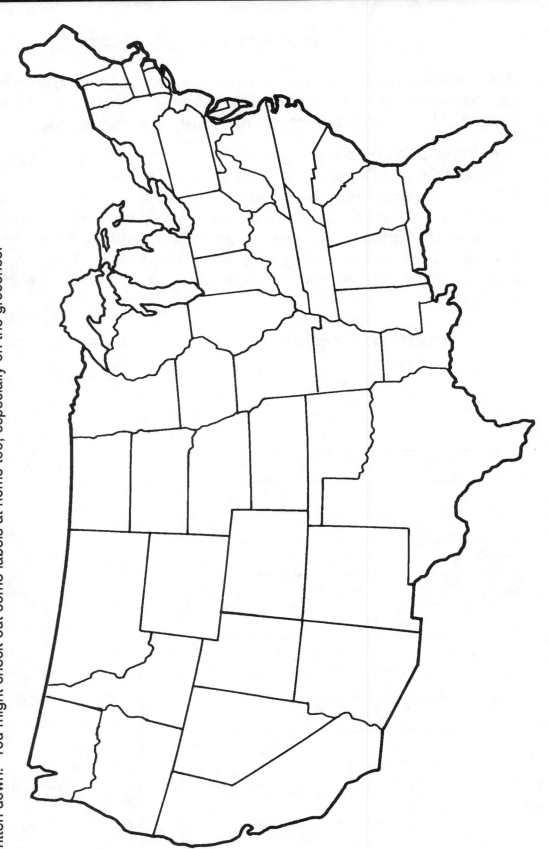

Working Out

See if you can do each of the exercises below ten times. Be sure to follow the directions carefully so that you do the exercises safely. Circle YES if you can do the exercise and NOT YET if you are not ready at this time.

Hopping for Balance

Hop on your right foot ten times and then hop on your left foot ten times. Can you do it?

YES   NOT YET

Touching Toes for Flexibility

Stand with your feet slightly apart and your hands out from your sides. Without bending your knees, reach across and touch your right hand to your left foot. Return to a standing position. Now touch your left hand to your right toe. Can you do this exercise ten complete times?

YES   NOT YET

Push-ups for Strength

With your knees on the ground, reach out and place your hands on the ground in front of you. Keeping your back straight, bend your elbows until your chin touches the ground. Can you do this exercise ten times?

YES   NOT YET

Sit-ups for Strength

Lie on your back with knees bent. Have a friend hold your feet to the floor. Place your hands behind your head. Pull up your head, shoulders, and lower back. Slowly return to your lying position. Can you do this ten times?

YES   NOT YET

Musical/Rhythmic Intelligence

Table of Contents

Grade Level Suggestions for Activity Sheets

Activity Sheet Title	Page	Grade Level(s)
People and Sounds	209	K
Sound Shapes	210	K–1
Nice and Ugly Sounds	211	K–1
Sounds	212	1
Imagining the Music	213	2
Musical Rules	214	2–4
Punctuation Performance	215	2–4
Book Jingle	216	2–4
Using Your Musical Intelligence	217	2–4
Music and Moods	218	2–4
ABC Poetry	219	2–4
The Maestro Plays	221	2–4
Rhyming Poetry	223	3
Safety Rap	224	3–4
Limericks	225	3–4
A New Tune	226	4

Musical/Rhythmic Intelligence

Description:

The musical/rhythmic intelligence is at work when we listen to music to help us relax or hurry up. Music is used for exercise routines, for marching, and sleeping (lullabies). Our ability to remember advertisement jingles is a product of the musical/rhythmic intelligence. When a person uses music to communicate feelings and beliefs or to express patriotism or reverence, it is also a use of this intelligence. Composers and performers are professional people who use their musical/rhythmic intelligence at high levels.

Students who are strong in the musical/rhythmic intelligence think in rhythms and melodies. They enjoy singing, whistling, humming, tapping their feet and hands, and listening. They learn most effectively through sing-along time, musical experiences at school and home, and by being involved in music programs (choir, band, instruments, etc.).

Development:

Infants are exposed to the musical/rhythmic intelligence earlier than any other intelligence. They are aware of noises and rhythms in their surrounding areas as early as when they are still in the womb. They show their first use of this intelligence during infancy when they make individual sounds and can even imitate different sounds and pitches. When babies are around a year and a half old, they start exploring tones by themselves without needing to copy someone around them. With the development of language comes the recognition of sounds and sequences in familiar songs. The development becomes a bit more widespread as children grow older. Some are able to carry a tune long before others, which does not necessarily indicate strength or weakness in the musical/rhythmic intelligence but rather a discrepancy in developmental speed. By school age, however, most children know what a song is and can reasonably reproduce fair renditions of common tunes of their society. After school begins, musical development drops off to quite a degree, depending on formal instruction. Some students learn to read music and understand theory. This is something that has to be taught and learned. It is not part of the natural absorption of music from the world around them.

Parents' Letter

Dear Parents,

We have all sung or hummed songs—whether they were nursery rhymes, popular songs, or advertisement jingles. This ability comes from our musical/rhythmic intelligence. Musical development begins when a baby is in the womb. Musical abilities continue to grow as a baby learns to make individual sounds and is able to imitate various sounds and pitches. Between the ages of one and two a baby begins experimenting with sounds without having to imitate anyone. A child's development of language helps him or her to recognize sounds and groups of sounds used together to express ideas. In many adults, actual musical ability is still being developed. Most people can carry a tune, but without more advanced musical training, this is where the musical intelligence will level off.

You might enjoy working with your child's musical intelligence at home. We will be doing exciting things at school, as well. You can help us by doing activities like these:

✦ Listen to music used in TV programs and movies. What kind of music portrays tension, excitement, turning points, etc.?

✦ Sing songs together as a family—worship songs, Christmas carols, show tunes, etc.

✦ Make up funny songs about difficult issues for your child. Let the songs include various solution options.

✦ Sing family rules to familiar tunes like "Old MacDonald Had a Farm."

✦ Practice expressing feelings and emotions with sounds only—no words.

We are finding out about so many different ways that we are smart! Thank you for helping us to develop our intelligence at home. It is so helpful to have families involved in the learning and development process.

Sincerely,

_____

(your child's teacher)

Teaching Students About the Musical/Rhythmic Intelligence

Chapter Five

One rainy weekday afternoon, Melanie and Roger were finished with their homework and were wondering what to do again. They had been having so much fun using their different ways of being smart, but they were anxious to find new things to do. They watched a program on TV about how people put movies together. There were all types of people involved—people who decided what pictures to take, people who took the pictures, people who talked about the pictures, people who put the talking and the pictures together, and people who chose music to match the talking and the pictures. This really fascinated Melanie. She loved to listen to music. Roger liked music too, but he liked music that made him jump, move, and run. After the TV program was over, Melanie decided to find music that would fit different ideas that she had been putting together with her words, numbers, pictures, and body. Roger saw what she was doing and decided to try to find some music of his own. Together they found some light, bubbly music to match their first snail stories. Then, Melanie wanted to find a slow, serious piece of music to show the time she had spent thinking when she was doing her scientific writing. Roger thought his science ideas were more fun than slow, serious music. He found some music that was loud and had lots of drums in it.

As they listened to different parts of the CDs their family had, they found a really low, sliding sound. Mrs. Burns said the trombone made those sounds. It made Melanie and Roger laugh. Roger decided that if the big snail they had found could make a noise, it would have sounded like a trombone. Then Melanie started looking for sounds that the little tiny snail might have made. She found the right sound, but the music moved too fast to match the pace of the littlest snail. Mrs. Burns said the flute made that sound. Melanie thought that someday she might like to play the flute and be able to make the flute sound like the little snail might have sounded.

They listened to all types of music. The jazz music they heard made them think of a party where a lot of people were all dressed up. They listened to some popular music that made Roger want to run, jump, and move. Melanie turned that off quickly. She did not like the noise her brother made with the music. She found some music that sounded like a little stream trickling over some pebbles. That was the kind of music she wanted to play. But Roger said he would go crazy with that on all of the time. They settled on a CD that had some wild songs for Roger to sing along with and a few quieter pieces of music that could help Melanie think about all of the ways she was smart. She was making big plans to tell the students in her classroom about the ways they were smart too. She was glad there were many ways to be smart. So far they had discovered quite a few. She wondered what the next one would be.

Mrs. Burns came back into the room. Melanie told her about all the music they had listened to and how she and Roger liked different kinds of music. She smiled again.

Teaching Students About the Musical/Rhythmic Intelligence *(cont.)*

"You're both musically smart," she said.

"Musically smart?" Roger said. "All we've done is listen to some tunes that other people have made!"

"That's right," said Mrs. Burns, "and the music helped you to each see different pictures in your minds. Music is everywhere in our lives. And we are all musically smart!"

"Wow!" said Roger. "I'm smart without even trying. I'm just being a kid, and I am already smart in five different ways."

Melanie started thinking again. She counted—we're smart in words, numbers, pictures, bodies, music, —we're finding out about the ways we're smart without even trying! I've been thinking about it so hard, and the different ways just keep popping out all over the place.

Melanie decided to give her dad a chance to use big words again.

"Dad," she said, "today we found out that we are smart with music. Do you have a different way of saying that too?"

"Yes," he said, "you have discovered your musical/rhythmic intelligence." That made Melanie laugh. She decided she had better start writing these words down in her book. She might have a use for them later. Dad agreed to help her remember and spell all of the different intelligences they had discovered. He was proud of his kids for discovering so many ways of being smart.

"But," he added, "you still have two very important ones to discover. I don't think it will be too difficult, though!"

Children's Definition:

Being *musically smart* means you can hear sounds around you, both in music and in other places. Whenever you sing a song or advertisement jingle, use music to help you learn, or sing in the shower, you are using your *musical intelligence*. Everyone is musically smart!

Activity:

Choose a tune you already know. Make up new words that will go to that tune which talk about the different ways in which Melanie and Roger are smart. You are smart in those same ways!

Other activities can be found under "Lesson Planning Activities" (page 199) and "Musical/Rhythmic Activities Across the Grade Levels" (page 200).

Lesson Planning Activities

The following is a list of activities that you can use when creating a musical/rhythmic lesson or when you plan to strengthen this intelligence. Use these activities in combination with those listed under other intelligences to develop a well-rounded curriculum.

- Ballads

- Chants

- Create Concept Songs

- Discographies (lists of musical selections to complement your curriculum)

- Environmental Sounds

- Humming

- Illustrate with Sounds

- Instrumental Sounds

- Listening

- Lyrics

- Mood Music

- Music Composition or Creation

- Musical Concepts

- Musical Performance

- Percussion

- Raps

- Reproduce Sounds and Rhythms

- Rhythms

- Singing and Songs

- Supermemory Music

- Tonal Patterns

- Vocal Sounds

Musical/Rhythmic Activities Across the Grade Levels

Sound Identification:

Have the students put their heads on their desks and close their eyes. Quietly walk to a different part of the room from where you gave your initial instruction. Make a sound. Students who recognize what sound was made should raise their hands and identify the sound. Examples of sound:

- hand clap
- bell
- sneeze
- cough
- knock
- hum
- hop

- door shutting
- pencil tapping
- running water
- paper crumpling
- pencil dropping
- snapping fingers
- sharpening a pencil

Song Writing:

After learning a specific concept, have students make up a song to help them remember what they just learned. It helps if you start with a familiar tune, like "Baa, Baa, Black Sheep," "Mary Had a Little Lamb," or "Twinkle, Twinkle, Little Star." Have students create their own lyrics. As they become more comfortable with the process, they might end up making their own tunes, as well. Rap and jingles are also catchy ways to help students remember a lesson's content.

Sound Band:

Let your class become a band without using any instruments. Divide your class into sound sections. One group might clap, another might sigh, another section can hiss, another can hum, etc. Decide on hand signals that will refer to the different sounds. Practice conducting the band. When the students are able to perform several sounds in quick succession, let different students become the conductors. As another extension, add gestures that signal students to make their sounds softer or louder. Over several band sessions you might increase the lengths of the songs you play and add diversity by mixing sounds together for different effects. You might wish to use the band to be background music to a story you read.

Name That Tune:

Help your students develop their skills in recognizing tunes and rhythms by playing "Name That Tune." More advanced students might be able to name a tune after hearing the rhythm clapped out.

Musical Rules:

After you have established your classroom rules, have your students put the rules to music. Use a familiar tune and write lyrics that will help them to remember the classroom rules. Do the same for school rules and cafeteria rules.

Accessing Musical/Rhythmic Intelligence Through Verbal/Linguistic Intelligence

Literature:

Poetry books and books about musical topics can be used in the musical/rhythmic intelligence area. Repetitive language books can also be used with percussion instruments to represent the repetitive vocabulary. Students can perform while the story is being read. Chorale reading and reader's theater are also good ways to access the verbal/linguistic intelligence through music and rhythm.

- *All the Small Poems,* by Valerie Worth: Sunburst, 1987
- *The Completed Hickory Dickory Dock*, by Jim Aylesworth: Aladdin, 1994
- *Now We Are Six*, by A.A. Milne: Puffin, 1992
- *Oh, What Nonsense*, edited by William Cole: Puffin, 1990
- *Piping Down the Valleys Wild*, edited by Nancy Larrick: Delacorte, 1985
- *Sir Cedric*, by Roy Gerrard: FS & G, 1986
- *Sir Francis Drake: His Daring Deeds*, by Roy Gerrard: FS & G, 1988
- *Spin a Soft Black Song*, by Nikki Giovanni: FS & G, 1988
- *The Random House Book of Poetry for Children*, selected by Jack Prelutsky: Random Books Young Read, 1983
- *A Visit to William Blake's Inn: Poems for Innocent and Experienced Travelers*, by Nancy Willard: HarBrace, 1981
- *When We Were Very Young*, by A.A. Milne: Dutton, 1988

Rhythmic Words:

Many words have a natural rhythm. When acted out, the rhythm might have nothing to do with the meaning of the word. For instance, the word "rhythm" itself is a smooth, flowing word, while "music" sounds like two quick hops. "Tree" sounds like what a lazy animal might want to do on a warm day, and "paper" sounds like two steps in a march. Have students listen to various words, not for their meaning but for their rhythm. Once they have practiced acting out the rhythms of different words, read a short poem or story and ask them to act out the rhythm.

Sound Effects:

While you read a story to your students, have them produce sound effects that might bring the story to life. You might read the story once through for a dry run so that your students can think about what sound effects might work. Then have a discussion about what sounds will complement the story. Assign different sounds to different students. Read the story through again while students accompany you with their sounds.

Accessing Musical/Rhythmic Intelligence Through Logical/Mathematical Intelligence

Graphic Music:

Give logical/mathematical students a method by which to hear music through graphs. Hand out a sheet of large graph paper to each student. Have them number from one to eight down the side (one number per line). Sing a note or play one on the piano (or other instrument) and tell your students that that note will represent line one. Next, play a note one tone higher. Have students draw a line up through one square to show the higher tone. Go one tone higher and have the students graph what they hear. Continue in this manner until you have covered an octave (eight notes). After your students have the idea, give them practice in listening closely to the notes you sing or play. Always give them a reference note at the beginning (not necessarily line one but maybe number three or five, etc.). Let your notes make patterns or other familiar objects on their papers. Move to wider ranges than an octave once your students have had practice with just one. Students in the higher grades might also begin to hear intervals (for example, jumps from note one to note three).

Brainstorm Music:

Develop with your students a list of music that can be played for various tasks, such as doing schoolwork, exercising, cleaning, and taking a nap. What are the differences among the music they have picked for different tasks? Why is some music conducive to some tasks and not to others? How is music used in life to help people accomplish their jobs (marches to help soldiers get where they are going, lullabies to put babies to sleep, etc.).

Musical Patterns:

Clap a short, rhythmic pattern. Start with something really simple. Ask your students to copy your pattern. Then change the pattern and have them repeat the pattern after you. After you have changed the rhythmic pattern several times and the students are able to copy your patterns, challenge your students to take turns in developing their own patterns for their classmates to follow or copy.

Ask your students to help you to create a code by which to write these patterns down. After you have developed the code, write several patterns down, using the code, and ask the students to clap those patterns. Let them write their own patterns that classmates can clap. As time and ability provide, make a connection to written music. It is a code, too, that musicians learn to read.

Math Rap:

After learning several math facts (addition, subtraction, multiplication, or division), have students use a few to create a rap that will help them remember these facts.

Accessing Musical/Rhythmic Intelligence Through Visual/Spatial Intelligence

Musical Montage:

From your discography play several selections of music (with lyrics) related to a topic you are currently studying. Write down the lyrics of some of the songs. Students can choose their favorite songs. Using old magazines, your students can cut out pictures that depict the lyrics of their chosen songs. They might also find key words that are in the songs to include in their montage. When they have a good collection of pictures and words, they can glue them onto a piece of paper. In the end you will have a collection of montages that complement your curriculum topic.

Music Advertisement:

Ask the students to draw a picture or a poster on which they advertise music. Why is music important? What would we do without music? This activity could be used after a discussion on reasons for using music. Armies use music to give signals and help soldiers get from one place to another. Politicians use music to help people feel patriotic. Music is played in elevators to help people relax. Advertisements use music to energize people, etc.

Musical Mobile:

Have students find pictures (or they may draw their own) of musical instruments and other music-related pictures to create a musical mobile. Have them paste their pictures on brightly colored paper and hang them from a coat hanger with colored yarn or string.

Seeing Sound I:

Let students know that the reason we are able to hear sounds and music is because the sounds are vibrations against our eardrums. Students can see how sound affects our eardrums by seeing how it affects other similar objects. Make a large model of an eardrum or have students make smaller models of their eardrums, using bowls or empty tin cans, plastic wrap, rubber bands, and rice or sugar. Create a drum by stretching the plastic wrap over the bowl or tin can. Secure the wrap with a rubber band around the rim. Place a teaspoon of rice or sugar on the plastic wrap. Gently tap the top of the drum. The vibration of the plastic makes the rice move as the plastic drops away from the rice and then comes back up with each tap. You might also find a way to make a loud enough sound to make the drums vibrate.

Seeing Sound II:

Another way to observe sound vibrations is by using a tuning fork and a bowl of water. Strike the tuning fork on a solid rubber object (shoe or mallet) or on the heel of your hand. Some students might see the fork vibrating. To make the vibrations even more clear, after striking the tuning fork, place it in water.

Accessing Musical/Rhythmic Intelligence Through Visual/Spatial Intelligence *(cont.)*

Displays:

Below are two bulletin board ideas to use to remind students of their musical/rhythmical intelligence.

Accessing Musical/Rhythmic Intelligence
Through Bodily/Kinesthetic Intelligence

Sign Music:

After learning a song, learn the sign language that goes along with the words. Sign the song. Try signing other songs your class already knows. If you are not familiar with sign language, have the students make up their own signs for the songs.

Model Ear:

Show students a diagram of the inside of an ear. Help them to understand that sound travels through the ear canal and up to the eardrum, which is a thin membrane. When sound hits the membrane, it causes the membrane to vibrate, and that is how we hear.

Let students make model ears, using the inside of a toilet paper or paper towel roll, a balloon, and a rubber band. Cut the open end off of each balloon (so that it will fit over the tube). Stretch the balloon over the end of the tube and secure it with a rubber band.

Ask your students to hold the open end of the tube to their mouths and touch a finger on the balloon. (*Note*: The finger should lightly press on the balloon's surface to allow the balloon to vibrate.) As the student speaks or sings into the tube, he or she will feel the balloon vibrate. Explain that this is how the ear works. The tube represents the ear canal, and the balloon represents our ear drum. Sound travels down the canal and hits the eardrum. When the eardrum vibrates, we hear the sound.

Freeze Movement:

This activity should be done where there is an unobstructed area in which students can move. A hidden music source is needed (so students can hear, but not see it). Tell the students that they are to move (dance, sway, march) to the music, but as soon as the music stops, they are to freeze. Those students who move after the music stops should sit down around the perimeter of the play area. Keep the music going on and off until there is only one player standing. He or she is the winner.

Paper Bag Band:

Give each student a brown paper bag (lunch size). How many noises can be made using a paper bag? You can shake it, tear it, pop it, crumple it, uncrumple it, and so on. You can change the sounds by doing those things quickly or slowly, loudly or softly. Let students practice their instruments for awhile. Then decide on hand gestures that can mean loud and soft and fast and slow. Each student should decide which sound (instrument) he/she will be playing. (If they are going to be a pop, they will do that only once, and then they will have to play a different instrument.) Discuss which instruments will play when the band is loud and which ones will play when the band is playing softly. Direct the band.

Accessing Musical/Rhythmic Intelligence Through Interpersonal Intelligence

Choral Reading:

Just like a choir sings a song together, your class can recite together. Choose a short story or a poem for your class. Divide it into parts where a few individual students might have a chance to speak; all of the girls speak together, all of the boys speak together, the whole class speaks together, etc. It helps if the students are familiar with the story or poem. Let them practice reading and saying it together. This is a great activity for a parents' night or assembly program. As the students get used to the activity of choral reading, you might take some of the stories the class writes together and make them into a choral reading opportunity.

Games:

Music recognition games, such as Name That Tune

Music creation games that begin with "Create a song about . . .

Rhythmic patterns and sound recognition games that begin with "Guess what made this sound."

Rhythmic pattern and sound creation games, such as *Going on a Lion Hunt*

Cooperative Groups:

The following list is from David Lazear's *Seven Pathways of Learning** in which he lists tasks for various members of a cooperative group.

Drummer makes up rhythmic patterns to match the beat of the stages of the group's work.

Singer thinks of songs or tunes about the group and the specific task it is doing.

Sound director helps the group plan appropriate background sounds for a report.

Composer makes up words for songs about the group and the assignment it is doing.

Volume controller ensures the group's noise does not rise above an appropriate level during a cooperative task.

Music coach leads group rehearsals for any musical parts of a report that is to be presented.

Rapper helps the group create raps and jingles about itself and its work.

Rhythm coordinator cues the group when it is to perform various rhythmic patterns.

Choral director leads the group in any musical or rap parts of a presentation or report.

Instrument manager gathers or creates the noise and sound makers the group needs.

*From *Seven Pathways of Learning*, David Lazear. Tucson, Arizona: Zephyr Press, 1994.

Accessing Musical/Rhythmic Intelligence Through Intrapersonal Intelligence

Biographies:

There are many people who use their intelligences to do great things. Listed below are well-known experts in their fields which would be particularly interesting subjects to research. For younger students, however, it might be more meaningful for them to see and meet someone who uses their musical/rhythmic intelligence. It is suggested that you use the list of careers to find an individual in your community who uses this intelligence in his/her workplace to come and speak with your class.

- Itzhak Perlman
- Linda Ronstadt
- Ludwig van Beethoven
- Ray Charles
- Robert Schumann
- Sergei Rachmaninoff
- Yehudi Menuhin

- Willie Nelson
- The Mavericks
- Lawrence Welk
- George Gershwin
- Joan Baez
- Zubin Mehta
- Ethel Merman

- Jean Redpath
- Gustav Mahler
- Leonard Bernstein
- Ella Fitzgerald
- Jenny Lind
- Stephen Foster
- Antonio Stradivari

Musical Feelings:

Ask your students to express various emotions through sounds only— no words. Have them experiment with different volumes, pitches, tones, and noises to communicate their meanings. Point out how people voice their emotions differently.

Software:

- Music literature tutors, such as *Exploratorium*
- Singing software that transforms voice input into synthesizer sounds, such as *Vocalizer*
- Composition software, such as *Music Studio*
- Tone recognition and melody memory enhancers, such as *Arnold*
- Musical instrument digital interfaces (MIDI), such as *Music Quest MIDI Starter System*
- Computer Systems Research Institute's *Menulay's Musicland*
- Warner New Media's *Music Exploratorium*

Careers:

- Advertising Agent
- Choral Director
- Conductor
- Disc Jockey
- Film Maker
- Instrument Maker

- Music Composer
- Music Copyist
- Music Teacher
- Sound Engineer
- Music Therapist
- Song Writer

- Performing Musician
- Piano Tuner
- Singer
- Musical Theater Actor/Actress
- Studio Engineer

Musical/Rhythmic Assessment

Musical/Rhythmic Processfolio Inclusions:

- Poems, raps, songs, or lyrics written by the student
- Audio or video tapes of musical performance
- Collections of curriculum-related music lists compiled by the student
- Observation records of instrumental or vocal performance
- Observation records of rhythmic and tune-keeping abilities
- Checklists for musical skill mastery levels
- Documents validating musical abilities (trophies, prizes, etc.)
- Concept songs and raps written by the student
- Reports of ability to discern rhythmic patterns
- Analysis of sound reproduction abilities
- Any record or product from musical/rhythmic lesson planning activities

Evaluation with Musical/Rhythmic Intelligence:

- Show rhythm perception in poetry.
- Demonstrate knowledge of . . . through a song.
- Create sounds to go with the process of . . . .
- Make up a song or rap about . . . .
- Make and play a musical instrument.
- Show understanding of lyrics as related to . . . .
- Identify sounds made by . . . .
- What sound would be made if . . . .
- Demonstrate understanding of . . . through a rhythmic pattern.
- Illustrate a story, using sound effects.
- Make a collection of music that can be used for various tasks (for example, studying, playing, dancing, and working).
- Compose music to express . . . .
- Do any activity that requires the use of music in response to an assignment.

People and Sounds

Circle the pictures of people using sounds and music.

Sound Shapes

Look at the pictures below. They are all pictures which show different sounds. Draw a **CIRCLE** around things that make **SOFT** sounds. Draw a **SQUARE** around things that make **LOUD** sounds. Draw a **TRIANGLE** around things that make **SUDDEN** sounds.

Nice Sounds and Ugly Sounds

In the top box draw pictures of things that make NICE sounds. In the bottom box draw pictures of things that make UGLY sounds.

 **Name**

Sounds

Close your eyes and listen. What noises do you hear around you? Can you hear birds, cafeteria workers, or students in the hallway?

Listen very carefully to one noise at a time. Make the noise with your own voice. What sounds make up the noise? See if you can write the noise, using letters. After you have written the sound, write what made the sound on the line next to it.

Sound   What made the sound?

_____   _____

_____   _____

_____   _____

_____   _____

_____   _____

_____   _____

_____   _____

_____   _____

_____   _____

_____   _____

 **Name**

Imagining the Music

Your teacher is going to play some music. Spend a few minutes with your eyes closed just listening to the music. What does the music make you see in your imagination? Concentrate on that picture in your mind. After you are sure of the picture the music makes for you, open your eyes and draw the picture here while you listen to the rest of the music.

 **Name**

Musical Rules

There are rules all around us to help keep things running smoothly. In the beginning of the school year, your teacher went over the rules for the classroom. They might even be displayed somewhere in your room. Write your classroom rules down. Next, think of a familiar tune to which you can write words for a rules song. Write down the lyrics (words) of your rule song at the bottom of the page. You will probably have to change the words of some of the rules to fit the tune (use your own words). If you need more room, you may use the back of this paper.

Classroom Rules:

_____

_____

Tune for Song: _____

Lyrics of Rules Song: _____

_____

_____

_____

_____

_____

_____

 **Name**

Punctuation Performance

We use punctuation to help us know where to breathe, wait, and stop while we are reading. It is important to pay careful attention to punctuation, and this activity sheet will help you practice doing that.

Think of a different sound for each punctuation mark. Write down the sound (or how to make the sound) next to each one. For example, every time you come across a period you may make a squeak.

, (comma) _____

" " (quotation marks) _____

! (exclamation mark) _____

. (period) _____

? (question mark)_____

- (hyphen) _____

Now read the poem below and make the sounds of the punctuation marks as you read along. You will probably need to practice this a few times.

**A little boy once played so loud
That the Thunder, up in a thunder-cloud,
Said, "Since I can't be heard, why, then
I'll never, never thunder again!"**
James Whitcomb Riley

After you have mastered this short poem, find other poems or stories on which you can try your punctuation sounds. Practice reading a story, using punctuation sounds until you are very comfortable. Perform your story for your classmates and again for your family.

 **Name**

Book Jingle

Think of a book you read recently that you really enjoyed. You are going to make a jingle to advertise this book to your classmates. Complete the information about the book below.

Title: _____ Author: _____

This book was about . . . _____

_____

_____

_____

_____

Write down the name of a tune you know. _____

_____

Now write lyrics to the tune, which tell about the book you read. This is like a musical book report. Try to make it as appealing as you can so that your classmates will want to read the same book! (Use the back of this paper if you need more room.)

_____

_____

_____

_____

_____

_____

_____

Using Your Musical Intelligence

Think of times that you use your musical intelligence or sound intelligence (musical/rhythmic intelligence). Write some of these times on the lines below.

_____

_____

_____

_____

Now use this information to create either a song or a poem about this intelligence area. If you write a poem, try to make every other line rhyme. If you are writing a song, choose a tune you already know or make one up of your own. Have fun and be ready to share your poem or song with your classmates.

_____

_____

_____

_____

_____

Name

Music and Moods

On the left side of the page, write some of the names of songs and tunes you know. Spend time thinking about each one in your mind. Hum it quietly to yourself. Think about how each song makes you feel. Do different songs make you feel happy or sad? Do they help you work or make you feel lazy? Do they make you think of certain people or objects? What does each song bring to your mind?

After you think about each song, write what thoughts it brings to your mind in the right column.

Songs	Thoughts
_____	_____
	_____
	_____
_____	_____
	_____
	_____
_____	_____
	_____
	_____
_____	_____
	_____
	_____
_____	_____
	_____
	_____

Name _____

ABC Poetry

Write a nonsense poem, using each letter of the alphabet. Follow the pattern shown. Try to make every two lines rhyme (A and B, C and D, E and F, etc.) If you have trouble getting started, try to pick a topic like animals, feelings, or objects.

A is for _____

that _____

B is for _____

that _____

C is for _____

that _____

D is for _____

that _____

E is for _____

that _____

F is for _____

that _____

G is for _____

that _____

H is for _____

that _____

I is for _____

that _____

J is for _____

that _____

K is for _____

that _____

L is for _____

that _____

ABC Poetry *(cont.)*

M is for _____

that _____

N is for _____

that _____

O is for _____

that _____

P is for _____

that _____

Q is for _____

that _____

R is for _____

that _____

S is for _____

that _____

T is for _____

that _____

U is for _____

that _____

V is for _____

that _____

W is for _____

that _____

X is for _____

that _____

Y is for _____

that _____

Z is for _____

that _____

 **Name** _____

The Maestro Plays

The Maestro Plays by Bill Martin, Jr. and Vladimir Radunsky
(Henry Holt and Company, 1994)

Below is a sample of the melodic style of writing that you will find in the book *The Maestro Plays*. Read this book to your students before completing the activities on this page and the next.

"The Maestro plays. He plays proudly. He plays loudly. He plays slowly. He plays oh-ly."

Bravo to the three maestros who created this virtuoso picture book!

There is Maestro Bill Martin who writes cunningly, punningly, winningly, grinningly, unsinningly.

There is Maestro Vladimir Radunsky who illustrates smartly, artily, grandly, and never blandly.

And there is the Maestro of the story, who amuses wryly, informs on the sly-ly, and encourages children to see how masterfully they can play with words.

After reading the book entitled *The Maestro Plays* with your students, discuss the use of language. The students might not understand the meanings of some of the words. Have them guess the meanings. Continue the discussion with the following questions and ideas:

♪ What clues help you to understand the words?

♪ How do the pictures and colors help you understand the story?

♪ Are all of the words in the dictionary?

♪ How did the author create the words?

♪ Imagine what types of instruments or sounds are causing the author to use the words he does.

♪ Note the rhythm of the words (e.g., flowingly, glowingly, knowingly, showingly, goingly, swingingly, flingingly, tingingly)

♪ Listen to a portion of a symphony. Have students choose pages from the book to match various sections of music.

♪ Ask students to brainstorm other word ideas that could be used. Accept imaginary words similar to the examples in the book.

♪ Ask students to think about the various sounds listed on the activity sheet (page 222). Have them write words that might make the same sounds (not necessarily words that *mean* that same sound, but words that *sound* the same).

The Maestro Plays *(cont.)*

After hearing the book *The Maestro Plays* by Bill Martin, Jr. and Vladimir Radunsky, think about the following noises. What words help you hear these sounds? Write as many words as you can think of for each sound. Invent some of your own words, too, just like Bill Martin, Jr. did.

RAIN_____

_____

CAR ENGINE_____

_____

BREEZE _____

_____

WIND CHIME _____

_____

BROKEN PIANO_____

_____

PROPELLER _____

_____

 **Name**

Rhyming Poetry

Write your favorite subject here: _____

Write some of the words you recently learned in this subject in the column below.

Now, try to think of words, even nonsense ones, that rhyme with the words you wrote above. Write the rhyming words in this column next to the words with which they rhyme.

_____   _____

_____   _____

_____   _____

_____   _____

_____   _____

Use the words above to write a poem to show that you learned something new in your favorite subject.

_____

_____

_____

_____

 **Name** _____

Safety Rap

There are many rules for safety. Rules are in the classroom, on the playground, on the streets, and at home. There are rules about fire, traffic, first aid, and many other things. Choose a safety topic, think about the rules involved, and then write a rap about the rules. Share the rap with others so that they can remember your set of safety rules too.

Safety Topic: _____

Rules: _____

_____

_____

_____

Rap: _____
                                            (Title)

_____

_____

_____

_____

_____

_____

_____

_____

_____

_____

_____

_____

Limericks

A limerick is a five-line poem that follows a definite rhyme and rhythm pattern. Read the following limericks.

Line 1	There once was a part in a play,
Line 2	A smart role, they all did say.
Line 3	A boy stood on stage,
Line 4	And like a young sage,
Line 5	Said, "Seven good smarts are the way!"

Line 1	He listed them all for the crew.
Line 2	He taught them to me and you,
Line 3	There's dancing and reading
Line 4	and listening and leading.
Line 5	"Now", he said, "you're smart too!"

Limericks are often funny. Try to make up your own limerick by following these rules:

1. Lines 1, 2, and 5 rhyme; lines 3 and 4 rhyme.

2. Notice when you read a limerick out loud that there is a strong beat in each line. Lines 1, 2, and 5 have three strong beats each. Lines 3 and 4 only have two strong beats each.

Try to create your own limerick!

There once was an old _____ from _____

Who liked to _____ on a _____

_____

_____

And now _____

 **Name**

A New Tune

Write your favorite subject here: _____

What did you enjoy learning about in this subject?_____

_____

Choose one of the following tunes:

Twinkle, Twinkle, Little Star

Row, Row, Row Your Boat

Mary Had a Little Lamb

Baa, Baa Black Sheep

Any nursery rhyme tune

Write new words to your chosen tune that will help teach a younger student about the topic you wrote above.

_____

_____

_____

_____

_____

_____

_____

_____

_____

_____

Interpersonal Intelligence
Table of Contents

Grade Level Suggestions for Activity Sheets

Activity Sheet Title	Page	Grade Level(s)
People Intelligence	243	K
Working Together	244	K
Color Hunt	245	K–1
Can You . . . ?	246	1–2
Story Sequel	247	2
Puppet Dialogue	248	2–3
Find Someone Who	249	2–3
Decisions	250	3
Interview Form	251	3
Which Classmates Can . . . ?	252	3–4
Create a Game	253	3–4
Career Interview	254	4

Interpersonal Intelligence

Description:

The interpersonal intelligence is at work when we discern and understand differences in other people's actions, moods, and feelings. This includes accurately interpreting facial expressions, voices, and physical gestures. We are also using the interpersonal intelligence anytime we are part of a team. Our ability to effectively communicate verbally and nonverbally with others is a product of our interpersonal intelligence. When we are able to influence a person or group of people by what we say or do, it is a direct use of this intelligence. People who use their interpersonal intelligence to a high degree are political leaders, teachers, and counselors.

Students who are strong in the interpersonal intelligence area think by proposing ideas to other people. They enjoy leading, organizing, relating, mediating, and socializing. They learn effectively through working with friends, groups, games, social gatherings, clubs, apprenticeships, and community events.

Development:

This intelligence begins its developmental journey with parental bonding. Very early in life humans start to recognize and accept familiar others (with smiles). As infants are able to imitate facial expressions and sounds, they learn to take part in social role playing.

Between the ages of two and four, this development continues as children develop meaningful relationships (friendships) with people beyond their immediate family members. In doing this, they learn effective social skills, exercising empathy and being part of a team. Our ability to recognize the needs and motivations of others without necessarily speaking with them (bodily language clues) is evidence of our interpersonal intelligence development.

Parents' Letter

Dear Parents,

We are all people smart—you can tell by the number of friends we have, by how much we enjoy playing and working with others, and by the ways in which we care about others. This interpersonal intelligence starts developing at a very early age as an infant recognizes his or her mother's and father's faces and voices. The development continues as a child starts adding other familiar faces to his or her favorite people list (brothers and sisters, grandparents, aunts and uncles, etc.). As a child begins making friends with people outside of the family, this intelligence area grows even more. It continues to develop as a child starts to recognize the moods and motivations of other people.

We are lucky to be in a classroom environment where we work and learn together. In addition to this interpersonal stimulation, we could use your help at home with the following types of activities:

✦ Do family projects in which each member has responsibilities.

✦ Play games that require communication, like "Telephone."

✦ Practice giving encouragement to each other, both verbal and nonverbal.

✦ Discuss family issues at a round table discussion where everyone can voice his/her opinions.

✦ Help an individual family member deal with a tough decision by brainstorming a list of solutions and prioritizing them.

✦ Role play options for solving family disagreements.

The ability to work and play with other people is an important one to develop. Thank you for your help at home. Your daily family interaction is very important in this intelligence area. Enjoy your time together.

Sincerely,

_____

(your child's teacher)

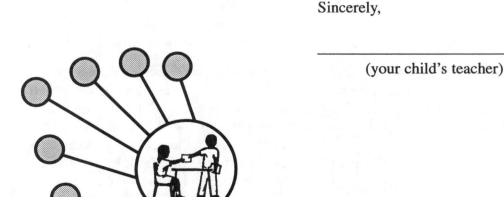

Teaching Students About the Interpersonal Intelligence

Chapter Six

The more Melanie and Roger found out about the different ways they were smart, the more the neighborhood children wanted to know. Melanie and Roger were happy to tell them about all the intelligences (Melanie remembered that word from all the big words her dad had used). The other children all wanted to know if they were smart in those different ways also. Roger was quick to assure them that they were all word smart, number smart, picture smart, bodily smart, and music smart. They thought that was pretty amazing.

This was another sunny day. There was not much homework that had to be done, and everyone was outside. They were all enjoying the break from the rain they had been getting.

Roger still liked to play with snails. There were not many other bugs as dependable as snails, so they had become a favorite for him. He suggested that each kid find a snail in his/her own yard and then come back to see which yard produced the fastest snail in a neighborhood race. That sounded like fun, and all of the kids decided that their yards probably had the fastest snails because there were so many (what they forgot to think about was the fact that all of the yards had many snails). After they all had searched for the healthiest snails in their yards, they went back to Melanie and Roger's driveway. They chose two cracks in the driveway and lined all of the snails along one of them. Melanie said, "On your marks. Get set. GO!"

They all let go of their snails and then sat back to watch which ones would go the fastest. Well, as we all know, snails do not go fast anytime, so it was a L-O-N-G race. Melanie, Roger, and their friends were becoming bored pretty quickly and soon chose a closer crack to mark the end of the race (at Roger's suggestion). Many snails went off the track and had to be carried back into place. Finally, one snail did reach the other crack, but no one could remember whose snail it was—they all looked so much alike.

So they left the snails to finish the race by themselves and decided to play other games. Melanie suggested that they each take a turn at choosing a game so that everyone could play games that they enjoyed. They had so much fun playing tag, and then hide-and-seek, and kick the can, and hopscotch, and soccer, and—well, they played all the games they could think of. Sometimes there were kids who could not agree on the rules, but somehow they all worked together to get problems solved without having to call Mrs. Burns outside for help. One by one, the neighborhood children were called home. They had not had this much fun in a long time. They all promised that the next sunny day without homework would be spent doing the exact same thing (except for the snail race).

Teaching Students About the Interpersonal Intelligence *(cont.)*

When Melanie and Roger came inside they were pretty tired too. They had enjoyed having a break from thinking hard about different ways of being smart. They had just had good, old-fashioned fun. Mrs. Burns winked at them.

"I'm so proud of you both," she said. "You discovered your sixth way of being smart today."

Melanie and Roger knew better than to argue, even though they both were pretty sure that their mom did not have a clear picture of what they had really done that day.

"You found out that you are both people smart today!"

"People smart?" Roger said. "All we did was play with our friends!"

"That's right," said Mrs. Burns. "I saw you all taking turns choosing games and sorting out disagreements with rules. The way you were able to help keep everyone happy and involved showed you are people smart!"

"Boy, it sure isn't hard to be smart anymore," Roger said with a grin.

Melanie agreed. She was feeling pretty smart herself. She could not wait to find out what her dad called being people smart.

When Mr. Burns got home that evening, Melanie met him at the door with her notebook.

"Dad," she said, "what do you call it when you are people smart?"

Dad grinned. "You have discovered your interpersonal intelligence," he said importantly.

Melanie patiently waited until he put his coat and briefcase down so he could help her spell those words. Interpersonal sounded pretty big to her.

They only had one more intelligence to go. Then she was going to go tell her teacher about all the things she had been learning about after school!

Children's Definition:

Being people smart means that you can work and play with other people. Anytime you do your school work with a friend or group of friends, play in a team game (like baseball), or in group games, you are using your people intelligence. Everyone can be people smart.

Activity:

Play a game with a group of friends. Afterwards, discuss how the game went. Did everyone play fairly? Did you have fun? Did you play by the rules? Did you make up some of your own rules?

Ideas for other activities can be found under "Lesson Planning Activities" (page 232) and "Interpersonal Activities Across the Grade Levels" (page 233).

Lesson Planning Activities

The following is a list of activities that you can use when creating an interpersonal lesson or when you plan to strengthen this intelligence. Use these activities in combination with those listed under other intelligences to develop a well-rounded curriculum.

- Board Games

- Collaborative Skills

- Cooperative Groups

- Division of Labor

- Empathy Practices

- Feedback (Giving and Receiving)

- Group Discussions

- Group Projects

- Interviews

- Intuiting Others' Feelings

- Jigsaw Method

- Peer Sharing

- Peer Tutoring

- People Sculptures

- Person-to-Person Communication

- Plan Development

- Role Playing

- Sensing Others' Motives

- Simulations

- Team Assessment

- Teamwork

Interpersonal Activities Across the Grade Levels

Games:

Noncompetitive games and activities, such as those in *Playfair* by Joel Goodman and Matt Weinstein

Communication games, such as "Telephone" or joint storytelling

Human interest guessing games, such as *What's My Line?* or *I've Got a Secret*

Working together in team games, such as relay races

Back Pats:

Have your students spend time practicing giving genuine encouragement and support to their classmates. The teacher might begin the process by modeling what is expected. For example, "Johnny really worked hard on his spelling words today. I know that was hard for him, but he really stuck to it!" Encourage students to reinforce each other's efforts rather than just outcomes or results.

Cooperative Groups:

In his book *Seven Pathways of Learning**, David Lazear outlines a list of tasks that an interpersonal cooperative group might have.

Organizer helps the group plan and agree on strategies for approaching an assigned task.

Encourager provides positive support and encouragement for the members of the group.

Motivator finds ways to keep each group member excited about an assignment.

Counselor advises the group on how to deal with any problems or issues that might arise.

Interpreter explains the meaning of any part of the group's work that others do not understand.

Involvement manager ensures that each group member contributes to the final product.

Taskmaster helps the group stay on task and makes sure that all parts of a task are completed.

Consensus maker makes sure that all members agree on and understand the final product.

Communications watcher guards the group's interaction processes (listening, hearing, and so on).

Paraphraser repeats what various members of the group are saying to help all understand.

Simulations:

Most students are very capable of creating as-if situations. Simulations can enable students to use the learned information in real-life environments. Simulations might be complex, dress-up, all-day events or might be mini-adventures in internalizing a learned concept. Teacher directed simulations work well, but students should be given the opportunity to create their own simulations also.

*From *Seven Pathways of Learning*, David Lazear. Tucson, Arizona: Zephyr Press, 1994.

Accessing Interpersonal Intelligence Through Verbal/Linguistic Intelligence

Literature:

There are many books that can be used in the interpersonal intelligence area. Books with the topics of dealing with other people and working with them cooperatively work well here.

- *The Giraffe and the Pelly and Me*, by Roald Dahl: Puffin, 1994

- *Grandad Bill's Song*, by Jane Yolen: Philomel, 1994

- *Here Comes the Cat!* by Vladimir Vagin and Frank Asch: Scholastic, 1991

- *The Old Man and the Bear*, by Wolfram Hanel: North-South Books, 1994

- *The Rat and the Tiger*, by Keiko Kasza: Putnam, 1993

Cooperative Storytelling:

Have students divide into small groups (three to four students). Read a story starter to the students. Let them know that when you are finished with the starter, they will be taking turns completing the story. Ring a bell, or give another signal, when it is time for another member of the group to continue the story. Let them go around, telling the story until each student has had at least two turns (one turn for younger students) to develop the story. When the story has gone around a couple of times, let them know that they should start to wrap up the story. When they are finished, have a discussion about how the process went. Did the other members of their group take the story in the direction they wanted it to go, or was it a constant struggle? Once they have practiced this activity several times (with different story starters), they will find that they are able to follow the same train of thought as the other group members. When they are able to work together to this extent, it is a true interpersonal connection.

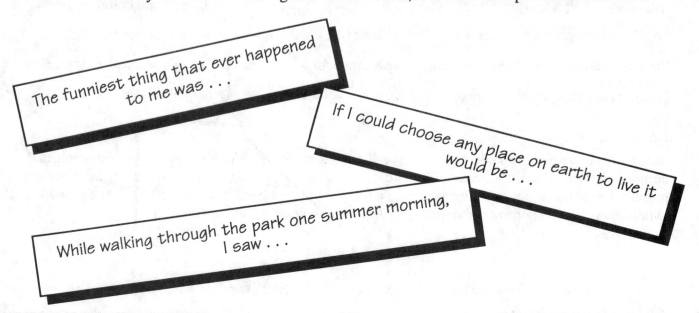

The funniest thing that ever happened to me was . . .

If I could choose any place on earth to live it would be . . .

While walking through the park one summer morning, I saw . . .

Accessing Interpersonal Intelligence Through Logical/Mathematical Intelligence

Group Problem Solving:

Any activity where students work on solving a problem or think logically in pairs, groups, or teams fits into this category. Working on math assignments together, putting a puzzle together, playing logic games together, and combining efforts on a scientific experiment are all excellent activities.

Code Clues:

Ask your students to create a code language that they can write down. Have them write a note to a classmate, using the code. A key should be included in the note. Then each recipient may respond to the note, using the same code.

This activity might be simplified by making up a class code first. Have the students write notes to each other using the class code and have the key easily visible. Once students have the hang of code writing, they might move on to develop their own codes.

Charting Individual Differences:

Have a discussion in which you point out that every person is special and different in his/her own way. Remind your students about some of the positive individual differences that are apparent in your classroom. Ask the students to interview classmates (lower grades might interview four classmates, while higher grade levels may interview as many as ten classmates).

Ask students to chart their classmates' names, hobbies, likes, and dislikes. When they are all done, you might incorporate the information into a classwide chart showing individual differences. (Students can use copies of page 249 to do their research).

Math Simulations:

Students can work together in a variety of ways in this section. Younger students might play shop where they work together in figuring prices and making sure they have enough money to buy the things that they need. Older students might do the same but add complexity by using checkbooks and balancing these at the end of every month (or week). They might also work on minibudgets together.

Let students start small businesses in the classroom (in partnerships or corporations) and think of all the problems they might have to overcome. (Minisociety curriculum works very well in the third and fourth grades).

Accessing Interpersonal Intelligence Through Visual/Spatial Intelligence

Group Mural:

This activity can be done either as a whole class or in groups or pairs. Students can create a display either drawn or cut and pasted to illustrate or show understanding of a curriculum concept. Groups can be divided up and assigned various tasks by the teacher; they might spontaneously assign tasks within the group, or they might just work together like putting a jigsaw puzzle together, where each person does his/her own thing to contribute to the whole project.

Reporters:

Students can work together to create a television report on a current topic of study. They may develop props and illustrations, and they can decide on a script together. Then, they can put the program together for a final product to share with the rest of the class, using a box with a hole through the side to simulate the television screen.

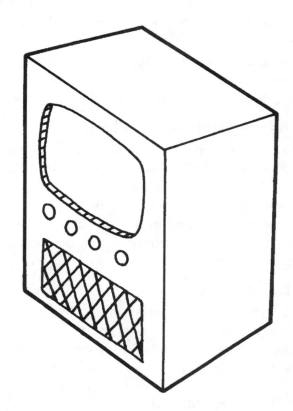

Reading Expression:

This can be done on an individual basis or as a whole-class project. On a large piece of paper, have students label a few emotions (happy, angry, nervous, excited, frustrated, afraid, etc.). Older students might pick their own emotions, while younger students might have just four simple ones. Next, have them cut out pictures of people from magazines and paste them in the area which best describes the person's facial expression.

Peer Encouragement:

Develop your students' abilities to recognize and act on positive things they see other people do. Tell them they are to look for good things that other people do. When they see something positive, ask them to fill out a form that reports the positive action or effort (stress that effort is as important as the outcome). Reproduce the forms on page 237 and make them readily available to your students.

Accessing Interpersonal Intelligence Through Visual/Spatial Intelligence *(cont.)*

Use these notes to encourage and recognize your students. Make extra copies available for your students to give to each other.

To: _____

From: _____

Date: _____

I think you did great when

_____

_____

_____

_____

_____

Don't stop trying!

Date: _____

Dear _____

I saw you when _____

_____

_____

_____

_____

_____

_____

_____

_____

To: _____

Hope you are feeling better!

_____

_____

_____

_____

_____

_____

_____

From: _____

To: _____

From: _____

Date: _____

I just wanted to let you know . . .

_____

_____

_____

_____

_____

_____

Accessing Interpersonal Intelligence
Through Visual/Spatial Intelligence *(cont.)*

Displays:

As a group we can . . .

play games

share

communicate

create

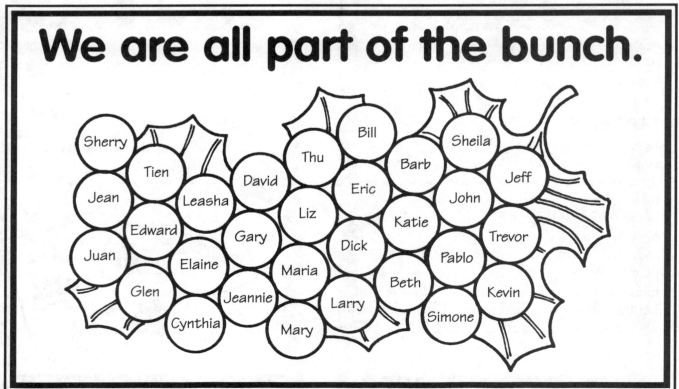

We are all part of the bunch.

Sherry, Tien, Jean, Leasha, Edward, Juan, Elaine, Glen, Cynthia, David, Gary, Jeannie, Mary, Thu, Liz, Maria, Larry, Bill, Eric, Dick, Barb, Katie, Beth, Sheila, John, Pablo, Simone, Jeff, Trevor, Kevin

Accessing Interpersonal Intelligence Through Bodily/Kinesthetic Intelligence

Class Actions:

Any activity which involves students moving around, using their hands and bodies, and working in pairs, groups, or teams fits into this category. Emphasize team involvement so that students can develop their abilities to communicate and work effectively together.

Student Mirror:

Have each student find a partner. One student will be the leader; the other will be the mirror. The leader will do motions which the mirror will copy. After a practice time, let the pairs perform in front of the class. The class should guess who is the mirror and who is the leader. The key is to move slowly enough to let the mirror join in.

Role-Playing Solutions:

Give nonspecific sticky situations similar to the ones that happen within your classroom. Ask groups or pairs of students to role play how to deal with those situations. Afterward, relate the role playing to real-life situations in which the solutions could be put to use in the classroom.

Relay Games:

Many classroom activities can be done using relay races. These can be outdoor sport races or indoor academic races. For example, students might team up and, in relay style, do different steps in a math problem or spell various vocabulary or spelling words. Reviewing social studies and science facts works well with this method. Being actively involved in teamwork is what makes relay races successful.

Class Plays:

Have students develop miniature plays about the content of your study. Working together will keep their imaginations stimulated. Being up and out of their seats for the activity keeps the bodily/kinesthetic learners involved. When they have their plays developed and their props collected, have each group of students perform their play for the rest of the class. For younger students more informal situations might be less stressful. Let them improvise their plays. Their imaginations work well, and the interaction will spur them on.

Accessing Interpersonal Intelligence Through Musical/Rhythmic Intelligence

Group Rap:

Some students can best illustrate and internalize what you have been studying if they have it in a musical form. Let students work together to create a rap. Let each group of students choose who will do the sound effects ("chicka-chicka, brrrrrr, etc.") and who will be the vocalists. Have them perform their rap for the class.

Class Poetry:

Create a poem, using the skills of the entire class. Have students call out key words in the current curriculum topic. Then have them suggest rhyming words for each key word. When you have the pairs of words, students can help to put it all together in a poem.

Song Puzzles:

As a class, pick a tune to which you will write lyrics. Divide the class into groups which will each create a part of the puzzle. Using a general theme, have each group take a part or section and write one verse for the song. When all of the groups are finished, have them sing the verses together. You will have created a whole song.

Guess the Word:

Ask students to find a partner. Explain that one partner is going to see a word (on the board or overhead) which they want the other partner to guess. The only clues they are allowed to give about the word are sounds (no words). The second partner cannot read facial expressions either (either blindfold partner #2 or arrange partners so they are seated back to back with partner #1 facing the board). Guessing words should be ones that evoke sounds, like emotions (happy, angry, sad, curious, etc.) or cultures (African, Native American, etc.). When partner #2 has guessed the word, have partners switch positions and reverse roles with partner #1 guessing and partner #2 sounding out the clues.

Careers:

- Administrator
- Anthropologist
- Arbitrator
- Counselor
- Manager
- Nurse
- Personnel Director
- Politician
- Psychologist
- Public Relations
- Salesperson
- School Principal
- Sociologist
- Therapist
- Teacher
- Travel Agent
- Religious Leader

Accessing Interpersonal Intelligence Through Intrapersonal Intelligence

Biographies:

There are many people who use their intelligences to do great things. Listed below are well-known experts in their fields who would be interesting topics of research. For younger students, however, it might be more meaningful for them to see and meet someone who uses his/her interpersonal intelligence. It is suggested that you use the list of careers below to find an individual in your community who uses this intelligence in the workplace to come and speak with your class.

Working together to find out more about these people will also develop the interpersonal intelligence. Students might each take a part of the research (for example, careers, where they lived, their families, etc.) and then come together, like pieces of a jigsaw puzzle, to form a completed project.

- Anne Sullivan
- Franklin Roosevelt
- Harry Truman
- Martin Luther King, Jr.

- Mother Teresa
- Nelson Rockefeller
- Winston Churchill

Software:

- Electronic bulletin boards, such as *Prodigy* and *Kidsnet*
- Simulation games, such as *Sim City* and *Oregon Trail*

Interpersonal Assessment

Interpersonal Processfolio Inclusions:

- Reports generated from group work
- Video or audio recordings of cooperative work
- Records of community service (letters, photos, certificates)
- Copies of letters to and from others
- Copy of a jigsaw project (a student's contribution to a group project)
- Records of empathy observations
- Evidence of ability to teach others
- Peer assessment records
- Records of interviews and questionnaires
- Evaluation records of random group quizzes
- Summaries of student-teacher conferences
- Descriptions of group projects completed and planned
- Any project that is a product of interpersonal lesson planning activities

Evaluation with Interpersonal Intelligence:

- Conduct a group survey to show . . . .
- Interview . . . to find . . . .
- Create an exercise routine involving several people.
- Explain to a partner how you would . . . .
- Create a story with a partner.
- Evaluate your partner's . . . .
- Argue one side of a discussion and then the other.
- Work together to create . . . .
- Create a play with your group to illustrate . . . .
- Paraphrase what you found out in listening to . . . .
- Take part in a simulation of . . . .
- Imagine how people feel when . . . .
- Solve a problem in a group by each person doing one step.
- As a group, perform an experiment to . . . .
- As a cooperative group, develop/create/explain . . . .
- Create a poem together that expresses . . . .

People Intelligence

Draw a circle around the pictures of people using their people intelligence.

Working Together

We work together when _____

_____

Draw a picture to show how you work together.

Color Hunt

Note to the Teacher: Begin this activity by having students color each item in the appropriate color.

Find people who can show you these things. Ask them to write their names under the items they can show.

Red Shirt

_____

Green Eyes

_____

Brown Hair

_____

Yellow Socks

_____

Blue Pants

_____

Black Shoes

_____

Can You . . . ?

Find people who can do these things. Ask them to write their names under the activities they can do.

Can you . . .

. . . sing a song?

_____

. . . count from 1 to 10?

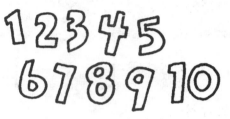

_____

. . . tell a story?

_____

. . . draw a picture?

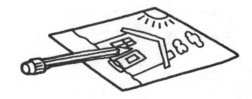

_____

. . . catch a ball?

_____

. . . enjoy playing alone?

_____

Story Sequel

Find a partner to work with. Think of a story you heard or read in class. You and your partner are going to write a sequel (part two) for this story. Take turns writing. Do not discuss what you are going to write. Write your own part and then pass the paper to your friend and have him/her write a part. You should each write two parts (total of four) for this story sequel.

STORY TITLE _____**PART TWO**

Friend A _____

_____

_____

_____

Friend B _____

_____

_____

_____

Friend A _____

_____

_____

_____

Friend B _____

_____

_____

_____

Puppet Dialogue

Choose a partner. Create two paper bag puppets (one for each partner). Decorate the puppets however you wish.

Now you are going to create a dialogue for your puppets. *A dialogue is a conversation between two or more people* (or puppets, in this case). Pretend your puppets can talk to each other. What will they say? Write your dialogue below. After you have practiced your complete dialogue, perform it with your puppets for the class!

Name your puppets!

Puppet #1_____   **Puppet #2** _____

Place of Dialogue_____

Dialogue

Puppet #1: " _____
_____ "

Puppet #2: " _____
_____ "

Puppet #1: " _____
_____ "

Puppet #2: " _____
_____ "

Puppet #1: " _____
_____ "

Puppet #2: " _____
_____ "

Find Someone Who . . .

Find different classmates who can do the following things. Ask each to write his/her name under an activity he/she can do. Do not have the same person sign more than one time.

Find someone who . . .

. . . can write his/her name upside down. _____

_____

. . . can tell a funny joke. _____

_____

. . . can sing a tune from an advertisement. _____

_____

. . . can count in 3s from 3 to 60._____

_____

. . . can draw a detailed picture of something. _____

_____

. . . likes to work alone._____

_____

. . . is often a leader in playground games. _____

_____

. . . can play a musical instrument. _____

_____

. . . can do a gymnastic or dance routine. _____

_____

. . . can retell a story._____

_____

. . . can put a puzzle together. _____

_____

 **Name**

Decisions

Read each sentence and decide how each person must feel. Write about the feelings on the blanks provided.

1. I saw Mary give Susan an apple from her lunch. I think Susan felt _____ because _____

    _____.

2. I saw Eric grabbing a library book from Ralph. I think Ralph felt _____ because_____

    _____.

3. I saw Joey win a race with four other kids. I think Joey felt _____ because _____

    _____.

4. I saw Chris get a paper with a low grade back from the teacher. I think Chris felt _____ because _____

    _____.

5. I heard that Bobby's father is on a business trip. I think Bobby feels _____ because _____

    _____.

 **Name**_____

Interview Form

Find a partner in the classroom. Try to find someone you do not know very well.
Use this activity sheet to interview your partner. Let your partner interview you.
When everyone has finished interviewing, share something that you learned
about the other person with the rest of the class.

Interviewer_____

Interviewee_____

Where were you born?_____

Where do you live now?_____

How long have you lived there?_____

Have you ever been to another country?_____

Which one(s)? _____

Have you attended this school since kindergarten? _____

If not, where did you go to school before you came here? _____

_____

Do you have any brothers and/or sisters? _____

What are their names and ages?_____

_____

What sports do you like to play? _____

What sports do you like to watch?_____

What shows do you like on TV?_____

What was the last movie you saw? _____

What is your favorite food? _____

What is your favorite subject in school?_____

What subject are you best in? _____

What was the last book you read?_____

What do you like to do after school? _____

Which Classmate Can . . . ?

Read through the following list. Think of classmates you think can do these activities. Write their names on the lines in front of the activities. Then go to each person you listed and ask him/her to show you that he/she can do the activity. Write what each did to prove it to you.

Which classmates can . . .

Who do you think can do it?		What did each do to prove he/she can?
_____	. . . count in multiples?	_____
_____	. . . draw a great picture?	_____
_____	. . . make up a song?	_____
_____	. . . do something unusual with his/her body?	_____
_____	. . . tell what he/she wants to do when he/she grows up?	_____
_____	. . . recite (remember) a poem?	_____
_____	. . . whistle a tune?	_____
_____	. . . be a good listener?	_____
_____	. . . show his/her feelings?	_____
_____	. . . make an origami (folded paper) object?	_____

How did you do? Did you choose the right people for each activity? Write about your experience.

Create a Game

With a partner or in a group, use this blank game board to design an original game. Think of a theme for your game. What will you use for game pieces? Will you need dice, a spinner, and/or game cards? Once you have perfected your game, share it with another set of partners or another group.

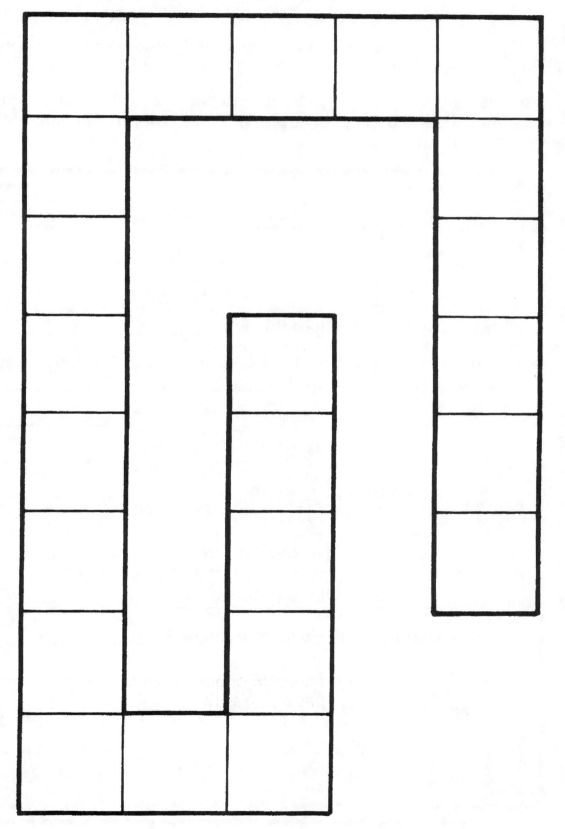

 **Name**

Career Interview

What do you want to be when you grow up? Brainstorm some of your ideas on another piece of paper.

Use this form to interview an adult who has one of the jobs you just listed. You may want to record the interview and fill in this form afterwards. Share your results with your class.

Interviewer_____ Interviewee _____

Job Title _____

Questions

How long have you had this job?_____

What did you need to do to prepare for this job (for example, schooling and training)?_____

_____

What hours do you work? _____

Describe a normal day on the job. _____

_____

_____

_____

What is your favorite part of your job?_____

_____

What is your least favorite part of your job?_____

_____

Thank you!

Intrapersonal Intelligence
Table of Contents

Grade Level Suggestions for Activity Sheets

Activity Sheet Title	Page	Grade Level(s)
Self-Intelligence	283	K
How Would You Feel?	284	K–1
Who I Am	285	K–1
Seven Types of Intelligence	286	K–1
Coat of Arms	287	1
How I Feel	288	1–2
Words About Me	289	1–3
When I Am Alone . . .	290	2–4
I Often Think About . . .	291	2–4
I Am Happiest When . . .	292	2–4
Feelings Graph	293	2–4
Things to Do	295	2–4
How I Used My Intelligence	296	2–4
Smart Planner	297	2–4
What's in a Name?	298	3–4
Personal Alphabet	299	3–4
They're Playing My Song	300	3–4

Intrapersonal Intelligence

Description:

We use our intrapersonal intelligence when we step back and watch ourselves, almost like outside observers. Our ability to understand ourselves, our feelings, thoughts, ideas, and perceptions, all involve the intrapersonal intelligence. Goal setting, planning for the future, recognizing our position in a larger order of things, and dealing with higher states of consciousness are all products of our intrapersonal intelligence. This is probably the area in which we recognize and practice spirituality, although Howard Gardner suggests that this (spirituality) might, at some time, be added as an eighth intelligence.

Students who are strong in the intrapersonal intelligence area think deeply inside themselves. They enjoy setting goals, dreaming, being quiet, and planning. They learn most effectively in secret places by having time alone, by working on self-paced projects, and by having choices.

Development:

The intrapersonal intelligence is a difficult one to assess in infants. When a baby first realizes that he/she is a separate person from his/her mother is when we first recognize the development of this intelligence. Development becomes more evident when children are aware that they have different feelings at different times. The ability to make correlations between feelings and the events that cause them is an important step, as well. Curiosity and concentration skills are the next steps in this process. Strong personal likes and dislikes and the quest for self-improvement round off the developmental process. Self-perception continues to evolve and change during our life spans. The intrapersonal intelligence is very personal and is outwardly portrayed only through other intelligences (writing, music, movement, etc.).

Parents' Letter

Dear Parents,

The last intelligence we will be exploring is our intrapersonal intelligence or our self-perception. We use this intelligence when we work alone. Setting goals and priorities is part of being self-smart. Recognizing our own feelings and identity are also a big part of this intelligence area.

This intelligence begins developing during the first three years of life when an infant realizes that he/she is a separate person from his or her mother and other family members. The ability to say no during the terrible twos is a milestone in this development. This intelligence is an area in which a person can develop for a long time by learning to understand the self, including such things as motivations, feelings, and ideas.

Your input at home can help your child develop in this intelligence area. The following types of activities encourage growth.

- ✦ Use different media (paint, clay, crayons, etc.) to express how you are feeling today.

- ✦ Games like *Concentration* and *Go Fish* require us to focus our attention.

- ✦ Create a meaningful personal symbol and explain it.

- ✦ Keep a diary or journal to express thoughts and feelings.

- ✦ Engage in activities that develop a positive self-esteem, like singing songs and writing poems about what your child can do right.

- ✦ Have imaginary conversations with people or objects that have caused upset and find solutions for the problems.

I hope you have enjoyed joining us in the exploration and development of our seven intelligences. Please do not stop doing the activities I have outlined in these letters. We will keep working with them in the classroom also. Personal development is a lifelong process. Thank you for being such a big part of it!

Sincerely,

_____

(your child's teacher)

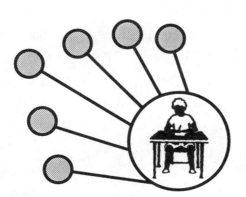

Teaching Students About the Intrapersonal Intelligence

Chapter Seven

After several weeks of discovering the different ways of being smart, Melanie and Roger were getting used to finding out about the various intelligences in the most unusual activities. They were still quite curious about the seventh way their parents had spoken about but knew better than to ask exactly what this last one might be. Mr. and Mrs. Burns were very mysterious about it, for some reason. Melanie and Roger knew that when they did discover it, both parents would be happy to let them know they had found it. In the meantime, they kept using their other ways of being smart. It seemed like no matter what activities they were doing, they were always using one of the ways of being smart. Some activities took more than one way of being smart. On another sunny day when all the neighborhood children were out, they all played *Monopoly*. They could see that the game needed them to use not only their number skills but also their people intelligence, to make sure that everyone was getting along and having fun. Another time, when they were not allowed to go outside again because of the weather, they spent the whole afternoon dancing to different kinds of music. The music used their music intelligence, but they were also using their body intelligence to help them move. On another really cold (but not rainy) day, they took turns writing stories and drawing pictures to illustrate their stories. They ended up with enough stories for a whole book, and the pictures were great! That day they used their word and picture intelligence. Even when they were not trying to be smart, they did things which later made them think of the intelligence areas they had used.

"Boy," said Roger one day when they had been talking about all of the ways they were smart, "it doesn't feel as though we will ever find the seventh way of being smart!"

Melanie did not feel that way. She knew that they had probably already used that last way of being smart; they just did not know exactly what it was yet. She decided to be very grown-up about it and ask, in a kind of sneaky way, about finding this last intelligence. Mr. Burns had the afternoon off and had come home early.

"Dad," she said, "will you take Roger and me to the library? We have some things we need to find out."

"What things, Melanie?" Roger wanted to know, but she gave him a look that told him not to say too much right now.

"Well, what information are you looking for?" asked Mr. Burns. "The library might not be the only place to get the information."

Teaching Students About the Intrapersonal Intelligence *(cont.)*

After Melanie had whispered with Roger to explain what she was up to, they both were pretty sure that they needed to go to the library. They said it had something to do with all of the different ways they were smart, and they would let Mr. and Mrs. Burns know that night if they had found what they had been looking for. Mr. and Mrs. Burns smiled at each other, and Mr. Burns said he would be happy to take them to the library.

When Melanie and Roger got to the library, they got out and asked their dad to come back in about an hour. He agreed, and they went in by themselves. Roger wanted to know exactly how Melanie planned to find out about the seventh intelligence (he was getting pretty good at using the word "intelligence"). She did not have a definite plan, but she knew that the library had all types of information, so if they just looked hard enough, they would find the seventh intelligence. This excited Roger. It was like a treasure hunt. And when they were finished, they would be able to tell their parents about the seventh intelligence. They would not have to wait for their parents to tell them.

Each child took a book and started to look through it. The librarian asked if there was anything she could do to help them, and Roger explained that they were on a treasure hunt.

"Well, not exactly," said Melanie, rolling her eyes at Roger. "We've been finding out about different ways people are smart. We already know that we are smart with words, numbers, pictures, our bodies, music, and our friends, but our parents said there's one more way we're smart, and we're trying to find it. Can you help us find where to look?"

The librarian thought they were already pretty smart, but she had not heard of these different ways and did not really know herself in what other way people could possibly be smart. She said the kids would probably find the answer in a way similar to how they had found the other ways of being smart.

Well, this really did not help Melanie and Roger, but they were not ready to give up. After looking through several books, Roger found a great book about different people and the things they had invented. He was fascinated by all of the different ways in which the people had tried to make things. They kept trying until they found what they were looking for. He spent the rest of the hour reading about these people and all of the things that they had made.

Teaching Students About the Intrapersonal Intelligence *(cont.)*

Melanie did not give up as easily on her search but finally also found a book that she just could not put down. It was about a group of people who wrote music. They did not all work together to write music; they just all lived during the same time in history and wrote what the book called *classical music*; Melanie had heard people talk about classical music before, and now she found out that all the music written during a certain time period was classical music. She read about the composers' lives, how they began writing music, what made them think up new songs, and many other interesting things.

After an hour, Mr. Burns came back to pick up the children. He had the same mysterious smile on his face that Mrs. Burns had smiled before. However, Melanie and Roger were too busy thinking about what they had read to notice. On the way home, they stopped to get ice cream, which was a real treat for the kids. They really enjoyed having their dad with them.

At dinner that evening, Mrs. Burns asked what the children had done at the library.

"Well," said Melanie, "we actually went to find out if we could figure out the last way we are smart. But the librarian hadn't really heard about all of the different ways we already knew about and couldn't help us. But, I had a great time learning about different composers. I always wondered where music really came from, and a book told me a lot about it. I found another one I'm going to read next time I go to the library."

"Yes," Roger said, "and I was looking too, only I found a book about people who invented all sorts of things. They were really smart too, but the book didn't say anything about being smart in seven ways. They just made some cool inventions that we use today."

Now Melanie and Roger noticed that both of their parents had that mysterious smile. "What are you guys grinning at?" asked Melanie.

"Yeah, what?" echoed Roger.

"Well, you don't know it, but you really did discover your seventh way of being smart today!" said Mrs. Burns.

"No, all we did was find some really neat information," said Melanie.

"But by going on that search all by yourselves and finding answers to questions you had, without our help, shows that you are self-smart!" said Mr. Burns. That was the first time he had ever said it in a way that Melanie and Roger could understand.

Teaching Students About the Intrapersonal Intelligence *(cont.)*

"Self-smart?" asked Melanie.

"That's right! Actually you've been using your self-intelligence all along. Whenever you think about what you're doing and ask questions, go in a quiet place to write your stories, or write in your book, you're using your self-intelligence. Today you made an effort to learn something on your own. That shows that you are both self-smart!"

"What do you call that intelligence, Dad?" Melanie asked, after she had gone to get her book.

"It's called your intrapersonal intelligence," he told her. Melanie carefully wrote i-n-t-r-a-p-e-r-s-o-n-a-l in her book.

"Wow!" said Roger, "I know; EVERYBODY who thinks and asks questions is self smart too!"

"That's right," said Mrs. Burns.

Children's Definition:

Being *self-smart* means that you know about yourself. You know what things you like and do not like. You also know what feelings you feel and what makes you feel them. Anytime you work on a project by yourself, ask questions like "Why?" and concentrate on something for awhile, you are using your *self-intelligence*. Everyone is self-smart!

Activity:

Think about what kinds of things interest you. What do you wish you could find out more about? How did you become interested in this topic? Where could you find out more about this topic? What are the seven ways that you are smart?

Other activities can be found under "Lesson Planning Activities" (page 262) and "Intrapersonal Activities Across the Grade Levels" (pages 263–268).

Lesson Planning Activities

The following is a list of activities that you can use when creating an intrapersonal lesson or when you plan to strengthen this intelligence. Use these activities in combination with those listed under other intelligences to develop a well-rounded curriculum.

- Autobiography

- Awareness of Personal Feelings

- Concentration

- Expression of Feelings

- Focusing

- Free-Choice Time

- Goal Setting

- Higher-Order Thinking and Reasoning

- Independent Studies and Projects

- Metacognition

- Mindfulness Practices

- Mood Awareness and Shifting

- Personal Application

- Personal Connections

- Personal Priorities

- Personal Projection

- Sensing the Emotions of the Moment

- Self-Identification

- Silent Reflection Periods

- Thinking Strategies

- Transfer of Learning to Life

262

Intrapersonal Activities Across the Grade Levels

Biographies:

There are many people who use their intelligences to do great things. Listed below are well-known experts in their fields which would make excellent topics of research. For younger students, however, it might be more meaningful for them to see and meet someone who uses his/her intrapersonal intelligence. It is suggested that you use the list of careers below to find an individual in your community who uses this intelligence in the workplace to come and speak with your class.

- Aristotle
- Emily Dickinson
- General George Patton
- Helen Keller
- Malcolm X
- Mohammed

Software:

- Personal choice software, such as *Decisions, Decisions*
- Career counseling software, such as *The Perfect Career*
- Any self-paced program (most of the programs in other intelligences)

Careers:

- Clergyman
- Entrepreneur
- Program Planner
- Psychiatrist
- Psychology Teacher
- Philosopher
- Researcher
- Spiritual Counselor
- Psychologist
- Theologian
- Philosopher

Concentration:

Exercises in concentration development help students with intrapersonal growth. These exercises might be as simple as playing the card game *Concentration* or as complex as Power Writing. (Students are given a choice of three writing topics and write for a solid three to five minutes without stopping. Writing time increases as their ability to concentrate on the topic and continue expressing thoughts improves).

Feeling ABCs:

This activity can be done over a long period of time (several weeks) or over a few days. With younger students it can go hand in hand with learning the alphabet. With older students it can be a separate activity. (Examples are on pages 264 and 265.)

Grades K–2: For each letter introduced for language or penmanship, have your students think of a feeling which begins with that letter. Ask your students to develop their own charts or booklets with these letters and feelings or to record them on a classroom chart.

Grades 3–4: Show several ABC books. Discuss their characteristics (each letter of the alphabet is represented, each letter has a word or words that it corresponds with, and each letter and word has a picture to illustrate it). Have the students work (individually or in groups) to create their own ABC books of feelings. Have them write and illustrate their books.

Intrapersonal Activities Across the Grade Levels *(cont.)*

Examples of Possible Facial Expressions for ABC Feelings

Angry	Disturbed	Guilty
Annoyed	Energetic	Happy
Anxious	Excited	Helpless
Astounded	Exhausted	Homesick
Bashful	Fascinated	Horrible
Bored	Fearful	Hurt
Brave	Foolish	Ignored
Calm	Frantic	Irritable
Confused	Free	Jealous
Curious	Frightened	Jolly
Cruel	Frustrated	Joyous
Discouraged	Glad	Kind

Intrapersonal Activities Across the Grade Levels *(cont.)*

Examples of Possible Facial Expressions for ABC Feelings *(cont.)*

Lazy	Petrified	Shocked
Left Out	Playful	Silly
Lonely	Pleased	Sneaky
Mad	Proud	Startled
Mean	Quiet	Tense
Miserable	Refreshed	Tired
Naughty	Rejected	Unhappy
Nervous	Relaxed	Upset
Nice	Relieved	Vicious
Overwhelmed	Restless	Violent
Panicked	Sad	Worried
Peaceful	Scared	Zany

Intrapersonal Activities Across the Grade Levels *(cont.)*

Choices:

An important part of an intrapersonal learner's day is an opportunity to choose. Wherever you can, work into your day an opportunity for students to make decisions about their learning experience. Intrapersonal learners will shine. This may involve giving students a list of assignments and having them choose the order in which to do the assignments or letting them decide on an order in which to visit various centers. Another option would be to offer a list of assignment opportunities that all meet similar ends but allow students to choose their modes of learning. Students who are not intrapersonally developed will grow as a result of these opportunities, just as exercise helps us to develop physically. This is true across the grade levels. It helps students to take responsibility for their learning.

Reflection Time:

Giving students time to reflect about their day or a certain lesson will enable intrapersonal learners to internalize their learning. This could be in the form of an informal discussion at the end of a period of the day or in reflective logs where they may do short self-reflections about what has happened. What went well during the time in question? What do they wish might have gone differently? What did they enjoy? What did they not? How can they use the knowledge that they gained? Walking younger students through this process will help them to self-reflect during non-guided exercises also.

Goal Setting:

Intrapersonal students are self-motivated. However, they need to have something to work towards. Goal setting sessions will help to fill this need. The forms on pages 267 and 268 may also assist your students in their goal setting.

Grades K–1 students might set their goals by deciding which centers they will visit during the day.

Grades 2–4 students can set short- and long-range goals such as which parts of a project they might complete during the week.

It is important for students to have a reflection time during which they can evaluate their goals. Were they realistic? Did they strive to meet them? Were they successful? This processing will help them to set realistic goals for themselves.

Setting classwide goals together is an additional exercise in which students can develop together. Go through the same reflection with the class after the goal time period is over. This will help to build class morale and develop their ability to work together and encourage each other (interpersonal extension).

My Goals and Activities for the Week

Use this form to plan your week. Check off each activity you complete.

Monday

☐ 1 _____ ☐ 3 _____

☐ 2 _____ ☐ 4 _____

Tuesday

☐ 1 _____ ☐ 3 _____

☐ 2 _____ ☐ 4 _____

Wednesday

☐ 1 _____ ☐ 3 _____

☐ 2 _____ ☐ 4 _____

Thursday

☐ 1 _____ ☐ 3 _____

☐ 2 _____ ☐ 4 _____

Friday

☐ 1 _____ ☐ 3 _____

☐ 2 _____ ☐ 4 _____

Things to Do This Week

Use this chart to help plan your week. Take the time to also consider what needs to be done next week.

Monday:	**Tuesday:**	**Wednesday:**
_____	_____	_____
_____	_____	_____
_____	_____	_____
_____	_____	_____
_____	_____	_____
Thursday:	**Friday:**	**Next Week:**
_____	_____	_____
_____	_____	_____
_____	_____	_____
_____	_____	_____

Accessing Intrapersonal Intelligence Through Verbal/Linguistic Intelligence

Literature:

Books that help students understand their feelings and the self fit into the intrapersonal intelligence area.

- *Becoming Myself: True Stories About Learning from Life*, by Cassandra Walker Simmons: Free Spirit, 1994
- *The Boy Who Loved Alligators*, by Barbara Kennedy: Antheneum, 1994
- *Gopher Takes Heart*, by Virginia Scribner: Viking, 1993
- *The Simple People*, by Tedd Arnold: Dial Books Young, 1992
- *Sunshine Home*, by Eve Bunting: Clarion, 1994
- *When the Nightingale Sings*, by Joyce Carl Thomas: HarpC Child Books, 1992
- *The World That Jack Built*, by Ruth Brown: Dutton Child Books, 1991

Journals as a Response to Reading:

After students have listened to a story, have them write in journals their responses to the story or plot. This can be done in words or pictures. Some responses might deal with whether they agree with what the character did in a certain instance or how they might have dealt with a situation differently. They might pick a character to be their friend and write or draw a letter to that character. Another option might be to give characters advice about circumstances in the book.

Personal Journals:

Explain to the students that they each will be making a special book about themselves in which they will express what they are doing and how they are feeling. Other people will not be able to read their books unless they are given permission. The books will show how classroom activities and their feelings change over a period of time.

Model the process of journal writing by expressing a feeling toward a specific event. If you are introducing the journals at the beginning of a school year, you might express excitement about the beginning of something new. Draw a facial expression that shows excitement and write why it is that you are having this feeling. Younger students can journal through pictures until they are able to express themselves through words. Encourage those who can to write even one or two key words about how they are feeling.

Complete the Story:

The activity on the following page is an excellent writing exercise. Ask your students to read the story portion at the bottom of the page first. Then allow them enough time to brainstorm ideas for completing the story. Finally, ask them to write the rest of the story and add a title.

Complete the Story

At the bottom of this page there is an ending to a story. Read the ending and then write the beginning and middle of the story. Do not forget to give your story a title!

_____

(title)

_____

_____

_____

_____

_____

_____

_____

_____

_____

_____

_____

_____

_____

When all was said and done, I had a pretty good day. I sure had learned my lesson, though. It's really crazy how a person can have such a scare and end up enjoying the day anyway. One thing I know for sure; my parents will never have to worry about me not listening to them anymore!

Accessing Intrapersonal Intelligence Through Logical/Mathematical Intelligence

Brainstorming:

Remind your students of the rules for brainstorming.

Brainstorming Rules

1. There is a time limit (three to five minutes). Stick to it.

2. All ideas should be shared.

3. No negative comments are allowed.

4. All shared items should be written down.

Lead students in a discussion about the many ways a specific thing can be done. For example, there are many different ways a person can help another person. Practice the brainstorming process with your students, using this and/or other topics. Other examples include the following:

- How can you decide who will have the first turn in a game?

- How can you keep busy when there is no TV and no parents or siblings are around?

- What kinds of presents can you give that do not cost money?

- What things can you do to show someone you love him/her?

- What games could you play with a blind person or with someone in a wheelchair?

Math Facts Self-Competition:

Give your students a miniquiz on math facts. Have them time themselves for how long it takes to finish. Give them similar quizzes periodically and let them see if they can improve not only in the time necessary to finish but also in accuracy. It is important that this activity be considered a method of self-improvement and not a race against classmates or neighbors.

Accessing Intrapersonal Intelligence Through Visual/Spatial Intelligence

Self-Recognition:

In a classwide discussion, identify things that grow and change, for example, pets, seeds, and babies. Guide the discussion into the subtopic of how we grow and change. What were we like one year ago? How were we different from how we are now?

Compile a list of questions and statements which will initiate self-descriptions from your students. Include such things as "How tall are you?" "Describe your hairstyle." "My favorite book is . . . ." "My hobbies are . . . ." Hand out the questions and ask your students to answer them. Explain that you will keep these in a safe place (preferably for several months or more). At the end of the designated period of time, repeat the activity with an identical set of questions. Encourage them to compare the first and second papers to see how they have changed.

Movie Endings:

Let your students watch a movie and then stop the movie part way through at a pivotal point. Ask the students to visualize and predict what might happen next. Let the movie play on and check their predictions.

Personal Mobile:

Using a coat hanger, yarn, and colored construction paper, have students develop a personal mobile. With pictures and words from magazines, have them show what interests they have, the things they like, those they dislike, what goals they might have for the future, what feelings they have experienced, and what caused those feelings. Tailor the activity to meet your classroom's level and needs.

I'm a Star:

Ask parents to send photographs of their children to school ahead of this activity. Begin the task by asking each student to imagine him/herself as a star. Ask them to think about why they would be famous. Then using the photos, colored paper, and magazine pictures and captions, have your students create billboards of themselves as stars. Allow them to be stars for anything from being a famous author or athlete to being a doctor or an actor.

I'm Proud of Me:

Have a discussion with your students about the things they have learned about themselves—their different intelligences, their abilities to deal with other people, their skills in problem solving, etc. Ask them to identify a few things that they have learned that really stick out in their minds. Then ask them to each design a medal for themselves, illustrating the single skill of which they are most proud. Use the blackline master on page 273 for this activity.

Other proud topics might include I am proud of what I did at home, I am proud of what I have done for my parents, I am proud of what I have done to save the earth, and I am proud of how I treated a friend.

 **Name**

Proud Medal

Design a medal for yourself. It should be for something about yourself for which you are proud.

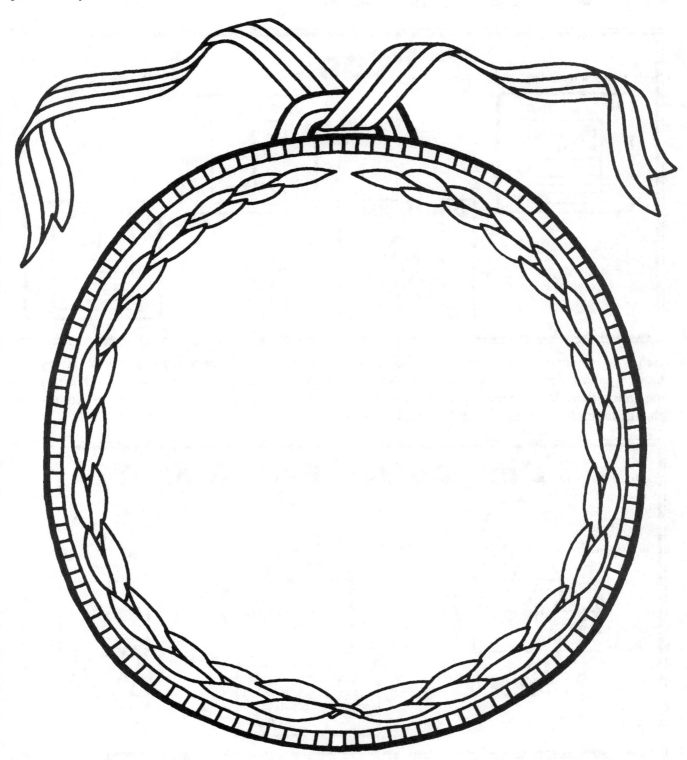

Accessing Intrapersonal Intelligence Through Visual/Spatial Intelligence *(cont.)*

Displays

Make a list of skills your students have learned recently. Let each child choose a skill he/she would like to demonstrate. Have them complete activity sheets demonstrating the skills. Display their completed work on a board to boost their self-esteem.

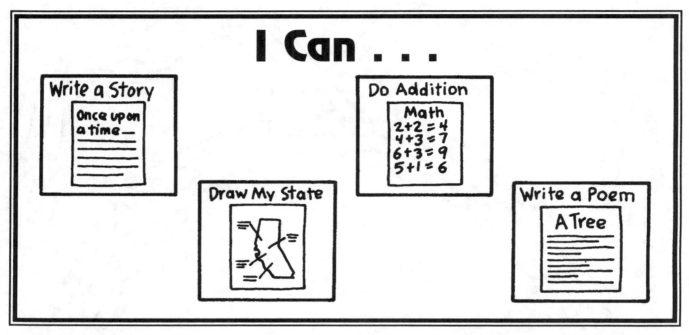

Help your students become aware of their feelings by using the bulletin board idea below. Every morning allow your students to place the clothespins (write a student's name on each clothespin) onto the appropriate flap of paper. Periodically throughout the day, give your students the opportunity to change their clothespins according to their moods.

Accessing Intrapersonal Intelligence Through Visual/Spatial Intelligence *(cont.)*

Displays *(cont.)*

Let each student have a section of the bulletin board in which each can display his/her own work. Ask students to display work from at least one of the seven intelligence areas.

Roberto	Ginger	Justin	Adrian	Daniel
Megan	Rick	Lucia	Adam	Sarah
Ron	Kathy	Kelly	Lisa	Julie
Chelsea	Jannae	John	Brianna	Holly

Accessing Intrapersonal Intelligence Through Bodily/Kinesthetic Intelligence

Acting Emotions:

Ask students, in turn, how they would act out the emotion of happiness. How would they act angry? Go through several different emotions, letting a few students act out each one. Point out that different people sometimes act differently for the same emotions. Discuss why and how this might happen. How would this affect them in school? How about at home? Sometimes people act in a certain way because they are hurt, but we might think they are angry. Role play different ways of dealing with the ways people act when they feel certain emotions.

Posture Talking:

Help students understand what posture is. Have them practice sitting and standing in various postures. For example, first have your students sit with straight backs and heads up and then slumped down in their seats with their heads up and their legs and arms crossed. Go through several similar exercises. Discuss how each position might express how a person is feeling.

Next, have students demonstrate different emotions in the way they walk. What would a happy walk look like? How about a sad walk? An angry walk? A tired walk? A frightened walk? Have your students walk any way they choose and have the class guess what emotion they are conveying (interpersonal extension).

Continue this activity by defining a facial expression. Ask the students to show, by using only their faces, how they would feel if they were sitting in the principal's (or a doctor's) office, waiting for grandma at the airport or train station, waiting to give a class speech or musical recital, at a baseball game when their team is winning and when it is losing, watching a scary movie, or watching a funny movie.

Exercise and Food Charts:

After spending time discussing the need for keeping our bodies healthy, have students record their exercise habits. Reproduce the form on page 277 or keep a classwide chart where students can work together to become more health conscious.

Discuss the importance of a balanced diet. Have students complete the information on page 278 and reflect on their eating habits.

Accessing Intrapersonal Intelligence Through Bodily/Kinesthetic Intelligence

(cont.)

Exercise Chart

How much exercise do you do in a week? Fill in the chart below for each day of the week. Some of the activities you could list include running, walking, riding a bike, skating, and participating in a physical game or a sport. At the end of the week, use the information in the chart to decide whether you exercise enough or whether you need to increase your daily exercise.

Day	What I Did
Monday	
Tuesday	
Wednesday	
Thursday	
Friday	
Saturday	
Sunday	

❑ I had lots of exercise this week.

❑ I need to exercise more.

Here is what I can do to improve my health by exercising. _____

_____

_____

Accessing Intrapersonal Intelligence Through Bodily/Kinesthetic Intelligence

(cont.)

Food Chart

Eating the right foods is very important to your health. Fill in the chart below for one day. Include all of the foods you ate. After each food, check (✔) whether you think it was a healthful choice or an unhealthful choice and why. (Use the back of this paper if necessary.) When your chart is completed, decide what you can do to eat right every day.

Food	Healthful Choice	Unhealthful Choice	Why?

Here is what I can do to improve my health by eating right every day. _____

_____

_____

Accessing Intrapersonal Intelligence Through Musical/Rhythmic Intelligence

Tone of Voice:

Just as we can express our feelings using our faces and bodies, the way we say things can express our feelings too. Model this by using an incongruent tone of voice for the message you are giving. For example, use an angry tone of voice to say, "I'm so glad you're all at school today." Use a happy tone of voice and say, "I'm very disappointed in the way you behaved yesterday." Discuss the message that comes across in these two instances.

Next, have your students practice using their voices to express how they feel. Let them take turns to use the following emotions to express the following sentences:

Emotions	Sentences
irritated, excited, jealous, happy, proud, annoyed	"I have a new baby brother."
excited, frightened, proud, ignored, jealous	"My sister is making so many new friends."
excited, disgusted, bored, left out, scared	"Our class is going to start playing baseball for recess."
proud, anxious, excited, worried, lonely	"My parents are going out, and I'll be alone at home tonight."
confused, excited, surprised, pleased, disgusted	"I got a shirt from my aunt for my birthday."

Ancestral Music:

Find out about the cultural heritage represented in your classroom. Ask the students to find out where their ancestors came from (asking grandparents is generally a good strategy). Next, have them find out what kind of music is/was popular in their country of origin. They can bring a recording of music from that country or come prepared to teach their classmates a folk song from their country.

Accessing Intrapersonal Intelligence Through Interpersonal Intelligence

Uniquely the Same:

In this activity, students will see that while we are all individuals, there are characteristics that we have in common. Ask the students to sit or stand in a circle. Call out a characteristic like hair or eye color. All of the students who possess that characteristic should step into the circle. Discuss how people with similar characteristics are also different. How are the people in the circle different? How else are they the same? Let those players return to the circle and call a different characteristic. Go through the same discussion every time. Be sure that each student has had a turn inside the circle at least once before ending the activity.

Games:

Exploring one's values games, such as *Scruples* and *Life Stories*

Self-analysis games, such as surveys and questionnaires

Mind expansion games, such as brain teasers or complex visualization journeys

Creativity games, such as those suggested in Roger van Oeck's *A Whack on the Side of the Head*

Cooperative Groups:

David Lazear outlined various tasks that can be used in intrapersonal cooperative groups in his book *Seven Pathways of Learning**.

Worrier is concerned about whether the group is doing what it is supposed to be doing.

Reflector helps the group think about the significance and implications of a task.

Processor leads the group in evaluating its thinking and cooperative behavior.

Quality controller ensures that the group is doing its best possible work and that the final product is good.

Feelings watcher pays attention to and helps the group discuss its effective responses to a task.

Learning awareness catalyzer helps the group be conscious about what it is learning.

Connection maker helps the group see links with other subjects, both in and beyond the classroom.

Concentration technologist suggests ways in which the group can maintain its focus on an assignment.

Philosopher raises questions about values and beliefs that emerge as the group works.

*From *Seven Pathways of Learning*, David Lazear. Tucson, Arizona: Zephyr Press, 1994.

Accessing Intrapersonal Intelligence
Through Interpersonal Intelligence *(cont.)*

Classroom Heroes:

This is a year-round bulletin board display in which students are recognized in turn for their positive behavior.

A picture of the student being recognized for the week should be placed in the middle of the board. Student (peer)-generated cards or papers showing (in pictures or words) the positive things the star student has done can be placed around the picture.

This activity might be reinforced at the end of each day during a few minutes of sharing about what positive behavior has been recognized among classmates.

Intrapersonal Assessment

Intrapersonal Processfolio Inclusions:

- Records of goals and plans
- Self-reflection exercise documents
- Copies of diary or journal entries
- Self-assessment checklists or reports
- Interest inventories
- Pictures and samples of extracurricular hobbies and interests
- Student generated progress reports
- Independent projects (or photocopies)
- Feelings/emotions processing (When . . . I feel . . . .)
- Autobiographical reports
- Concentration tests and results
- Any product from intrapersonal lesson planning activities

Evaluation with Intrapersonal Intelligence:

- Tell what you can do to improve . . . .
- Describe how you feel when . . . .
- If you were a character in (a book, movie) . . . what would you do?
- What's your opinion on . . . ?
- Write a journal entry about . . . .
- Tell how you will use . . . (curriculum content) outside of school.
- Tell how an event in . . . (history, literature, science) is similar to an experience you have had.
- Explain how your life would be different if . . . .
- Write about how you would . . . .
- Plan and complete a project about . . . by yourself.
- Create a product (art) that shows . . . .
- Include any activity that requires the use of intrapersonal capacities in response to an assignment.

Self-Intelligence

Circle the pictures of people using their self-intelligence.

Name _____

How Would You Feel?

In the corners, draw faces of how you would feel if these things happened to you.

Name

Who I Am

Cut out from a magazine pictures that would help others to know you better (think of things and activities you like). Glue them onto this page.

Seven Types of Intelligence

Draw pictures to show times when you have used each of your intelligences.

WORD

PEOPLE

NUMBER

SELF

SOUND

PICTURE

BODY

286

Coat of Arms

Make your own coat of arms on the picture below.

- ❖ In space 1, draw a picture of your family.
- ❖ In space 2, draw a picture of your favorite hobby.
- ❖ In space 3, draw a picture of your favorite book and character.
- ❖ In space 4, draw a picture of something new you would like to do in your lifetime.

 **Name**

How I Feel

Be aware of your feelings during the day by writing words or drawing pictures of how you feel at different times.

Time of Day	How I Feel
Start of School	
Recess Time	
Lunch Time	
End of School	

 **Name**

Words About Me

If you were to meet someone who needed to know you very well in a short amount of time, how would you tell that stranger about yourself? Use the chalkboard and the lines below to write words and phrases which would help the person know you in a hurry.

When I Am Alone . . .

Complete the following phrase with a picture or with writing.

When I am alone I like to . . .

290

I Often Think About . . .

Complete the following phrase with a picture or with writing.

I often think about . . .

I Am Happiest When . . .

Complete the following phrase with a picture or with writing.

I am happiest when . . .

Feelings Graph

Think about your feelings during the day. Complete this graph every 45 minutes, starting at the bottom of the graph. Mark HOW you feel by placing an X in the box. Think about WHY you feel that way and write a word or a phrase that will help you remember why. Do this activity for about three days (you will need several copies). Use page 294 to help you understand your feelings.

2:45			
2:00			
1:15			
12:30			
11:45			
11:00			
10:15			
9:30			
8:45			
8:00			

☺   😐   ☹

Feelings Graph *(cont.)*

Note to the Teacher: It might be helpful to work through this sheet together. Each student will be comparing his or her own charts, but you might explain the steps orally and possibly give examples to help students understand what they are looking for. Give students sufficient time to respond before reading the next instructions.

After keeping your feelings graph for several days, compare the graphs. Fill in this activity sheet to help you understand your feelings and what causes them.

Are your graphs very *similar* or very *different?* (circle one)

Did you feel different feelings when similar things happened? Explain.

_____

_____

_____

Look at each chart at the same time (check all of the 8:00 times, then all of the 8:45 times, and so on). Were there times when you felt very close to the same feelings at the same time of the day?_____

_____

_____

What do you think the reason for this is?_____

_____

Look at the times during the days when you were feeling your worst. Check your notes to see what your reasons for feeling bad were. Is there something you could change or do so that you could feel better about what was happening? Explain. _____

_____

_____

_____

Now that you know WHY you feel different feelings, keep a feelings graph for another several days. Be aware of your feelings and find ways to try to prevent yourself from feeling bad.

Name

Things to Do

When you think about and make notes about the things you need to do, it often helps you to get them done. Use this page to help you organize your thoughts so that you can keep up with your work. Add and change what you write here as often as you need to. Cross off things as you get them done. Do not forget to transfer unfinished tasks to your new goal sheet when you start your next one.

Things to Do Today

_____   _____

_____   _____

_____   _____

Things to Do Tomorrow

_____   _____

_____   _____

_____   _____

Things to Get Done This Week

_____   _____

_____   _____

_____   _____

Projects for This Month

_____   _____

_____   _____

_____   _____

Future Projects to Think About

_____   _____

_____   _____

Name _____

How I Used My Intelligence

Think about this past week. You have used each of your intelligences during the week. Now make a note or draw a picture of times when you used each of these intelligences.

I drew a picture to show ...	I used numbers to ...

I worked in a group when ...	I sang a song (or hummed) when ...

I used words to tell a friend about ...	I used my body when ...

Name

Smart Planner

Plan your week. Try to use a different way of being smart each day. Make a note of things to try in each area.

	Draw a picture to show which intelligence you will use each day.	Write or draw different ways you will use each Intelligence.
MON.		
TUE.		
WED.		
THUR.		
FRI.		

What's in a Name?

Write your first name down the left side of the paper. Using each letter in your name, write statements about yourself. Then do the same thing with your last name on the right side of the paper. Use the back side of this paper if you need more room. See the example below for an idea.

> **M**—Makes things with paper
>
> **E**—Enjoys sewing
>
> **G**—Gets along well with others
>
> **A**—Always speaks her mind
>
> **N**—Never gives up

First Name	**Last Name**
____ _____	____ _____
____ _____	____ _____
____ _____	____ _____
____ _____	____ _____
____ _____	____ _____
____ _____	____ _____
____ _____	____ _____
____ _____	____ _____

Name

Personal Alphabet

Write a word or statement about yourself, using each letter of the alphabet.

A: _____

B: _____

C: _____

D: _____

E: _____

F: _____

G: _____

H: _____

I: _____

J: _____

K: _____

L: _____

M: _____

N: _____

O: _____

P: _____

Q: _____

R: _____

S: _____

T: _____

U: _____

V: _____

W: _____

X: _____

Y: _____

Z: _____

They're Playing My Song

Help someone get to know you better by telling about yourself in a song.

Think of five things that you want people to know about you.

_____

_____

_____

_____

_____

Name a favorite or familiar song or tune that you know.

_____

_____

Now, using the characteristics listed above, rewrite them so that they fit in the tune you chose.

_____

_____

_____

_____

_____

_____

_____

_____

Related Resources

Verbal/Linguistic

Ashton-Warner, Sylvia. *Teacher.* Simon and Schuster, 1986.

Bissex, Glenda. *Genius at Work: A Child Learns to Write and Read.* Harvard University Press, 1980.

Bryant, Margaret, Marjorie Keiper, and Anne Petit. *Month by Month with Children's Literature: Your K–3 Curriculum for Mathmatics, Science, Social Studies, and More.* Zephyr Press, 1994.

Graves, Donald, and Virginia Stuart. *Write from the Start: Tapping Your Child's Natural Writing Ability.* NAL, 1987.

Johnson, Katie. *More Than Words: Child-Centered Lessons for Connecting Life and Literacy.* Zephyr Press, 1994.

Rico, Gabrielle Lusse. *Writing the Natural Way.* J. P. Tarcher, 1983.

Rose, Laura. *Write to Read and Spell: Teaching the Basics Through a Whole-Language Journal Program.* Zephyr Press, 1994.

Trelease, Jim. *The Read-Aloud Handbook.* Penguin, 1982.

Logical/Mathematical

Burns, Marilyn. *The I Hate Mathematics! Book.* Little, Brown, and Co., 1975.

Lorton, Mary Baratta. *Mathematics Their Way.* Addison-Wesley, 1976.

Patterns in Puzzles. Zephyr Press, 1992. (Puzzles for Grades 3–12).

Ready or Not. Zephyr Press, 1994. (Board Game for Grades 3–12).

Visual/ Spatial

DeMille, Richard. *Put Your Mother on the Ceiling: Children's Imagination Games.* Santa Barbara Press, 1981.

Edwards, Betty. *Drawing on the Right Side of the Brain.* J. P. Tarcher, 1979.

The Magic 7: Tools to Build Your Multiple Intelligences. Zephyr Press, 1995. (interactive comic books which teach students about their intelligences)

Pablo. Zephyr Press. (plastic connectors for 3-D sculptures)

Rose, Laura. *Folktales Audiotapes: Teaching Reading Through Visualization and Drawing.* Zephyr Press, 1992.

Rose, Laura. *Folktales: Teaching Reading Through Visualization and Drawing.* Zephyr Press, 1992.

Warner, Sally. *Encouraging the Artist in Your Child.* St. Martin's Press, 1989.

Related Resources *(cont.)*

Bodily/Kinesthetic

Benzwie, Teresa. *A Moving Experience: Dance for Lovers of Children and the Child Within.* Zephyr Press, 1988.

Cobb, Vicki. *Science Experiments You Can Eat.* Lippincott, 1972.

Gilbert, Anne G. *Teaching the 3 R's Through Movement Experiences.* Macmillan, 1977.

Hannaford, Carla, Cherokee Shaner, and Sandra Zachary. *Education in Motion: A Practical Guide to Whole-Brain Body Integration for Everyone.* Zephyr Press, 1993

Herman, Gail Neary, and Patricia Hollingsworth. *Kinetic Kaleidoscope: Activities for Exploring Movement and Energy in the Visual Arts.* Zephyr Press, 1992.

Schneider, Tom. *Everybody's a Winner: A Kid's Guide to New Sports and Fitness.* Little, Brown, and Co., 1976.

Spolin, Viola. *Theater Games for the Classroom.* Northwestern University Press, 1986.

Musical/Rhythmic

Bonny, Helen and Louis Savary. *Music and Your Mind.* Station Hill Press, 1990.

Brewer, Chris Boyd and Don G. Campbell. *Rhythms of Learning.* Zephyr Press, 1991.

Halpern, Steven, and Savary Louis. *Sound Health: Music and Sounds That Make Us Whole.* Harper and Row, 1985.

Judy, Stephanie. *Making Music for the Joy of It.* J. P. Tarcher, 1990.

Merritt, Stephanie. *Mind, Music, and Imagery: 40 Exercises Using Music to Stimulate Creativity and Self-Awareness.* NAL/Plume, 1990.

Wallace, Roeslla R. *Rappin' and Rhymin': Raps, Songs, Cheers, and Smart Rope Jingles for Active Learning.* Zephyr Press, 1992.

Related Resources *(cont.)*

Interpersonal

Johnson, David W., Roger T. Johnson, and Edythe Johnson Holubed. *Circles of Learning: Cooperation in the Classroom.* Association for Supervision and Curriculum Development, 1986.

Leff, Herbert L. and Ann Nevin. *Turning Learning Inside Out: A Guide for Using Any Subject to Enrich Life and Creativity.* Zephyr Press, 1994.

Orlick, Terry. *The Cooperative Sports and Games Book.* Pantheon, 1978.

Putte, Katherine Ruggieri-Vande. *Our Town: A Simulation of Contemporary Community Issues.* Zephyr Press, 1995

Sobel, Jeffrey. *Everybody Wins: 393 Non-Competitive Games for Young Children.* Walker and Co., 1983.

Wade, Rhima Carol. *Joining Hands: From Personal to Planetary Friendship in the Primary Classroom.* Zephyr Press, 1991.

Intrapersonal

Armstrong, Thomas. *The Radiant Child.* Quest, 1985.

Briggs, Dorothy Corkille. *Your Child's Self-Esteem.* Doubleday, 1970.

Canfield, Fack and Harold C. Wells. *100 Ways to Enhance Self-Esteem in the Classroom.* Prentice-Hall, 1976.

Gibbons, Maurice. *How to Become an Expert: Discover, Research, and Build a Project in Your Chosen Field.* Zephyr Press, 1991.

Gordon, Noah. *Magical Classroom: Creating Effective, Brain-Friendly Environments for Learning.* Zephyr Press, 1995.

Udall, Anne J. and Joan E. Daniels. *Creating the Thoughtful Classroom: Strategies to Promote Student Thinking.* Zephyr Press, 1991.

Wilson, Leslie Owen. *Every Child, Whole Child: Classroom Activities for Unleashing Natural Abilities.* Zephyr Press, 1994.

Multiple Intelligence Resources

Armstrong, Thomas. *In Their Own Way: Discovering and Encouraging Your Child's Personal Learning Style.* J. P. Tarcher; St. Martin's Press, 1987.

Armstrong, Thomas. *Multiple Intelligences in the Classroom.* Association for Supervision and Curriculum Development, 1994.

Armstrong, Thomas. *7 Kinds of Smart: Discovering and Using Your Natural Intelligences.* Plume/Penguin, 1993.

Bruestch, Anne. *Multiple Intelligence Lesson Plan Book.* Zephyr Press, 1995.

Campbell, Bruce. *Multiple Intelligences Handbook.* Campbell & Associates, Inc., 1994.

Campbell, Linda, Bruce Campbell, and Dee Dickinson. *Teaching and Learning Through Multiple Intelligences.* Zephyr Press, 1993.

Gardner, Howard. *Frames of Mind: The Theory of Multiple Intelligences.* Basic Books, 1983.

Gardner, Howard. *Multiple Intelligences: The Theory in Practice.* Basic Books, 1993.

Lazear, David. *Multiple Intelligence Approaches to Assessment: Solving the Assessment Conundrum.* Zephyr Press, 1994.

Lazear, David. *Seven Pathways of Learning: Teaching Students and Parents about Multiple Intelligences.* Zephyr Press, 1994.

Lazear, David. *Seven Ways of Knowing: Teaching for Multiple Intelligences.* Skylight, 1991.

Lazear, David. *Seven Ways of Teaching: The Artistry of Teaching with Multiple Intelligences.* Skylight, 1991.

Teele, Sue. *Teaching and Assessment Strategies Appropriate for the Multiple Intelligences.* University of California Extension, 1991.

Thornburg, David. *The Role of Technology in Teaching to the Whole Child: Multiple Intelligences in the Classroom.* Starsong Publications, 1989.